MW01716565

Microsoft Word® Quick Reference

Bryan L. Pfaffenberger

QUE

Microsoft Word Quick Reference.

Library of Congress Catalog Number:

ISBN 0-88022-720-6

94 93 92 91 4 3 2 1

Interpretation of the printing code: the rightmost double-digit number is the year of the book's printing; the rightmost single-digit number is the number of the book's printing. For example, a printing code of 91-1 shows that the first printing of the book occurred in 1991.

This book is based on Microsoft Word Version 5.5.

Que Quick Reference Series

The *Que Quick Reference Series* is a portable resource of essential microcomputer knowledge. Whether you are a new or experienced user, you can rely on the high-quality information contained in these convenient guides.

Drawing on the experience of many of Que's best-selling authors, the *Que Quick Reference Series* helps you easily access important program information.

The *Que Quick Reference Series* includes these titles:

1-2-3 Quick Reference
1-2-3 Release 2.2 Quick Reference
1-2-3 Release 3 Quick Reference
1-2-3 Release 3.1 Quick Reference
Allways Quick Reference
Assembly Language Quick Reference
AutoCAD Quick Reference, 2nd Edition
C Quick Reference
CorelDRAW Quick Reference
dBASE IV Quick Reference
DOS and BIOS Functions Quick Reference
Excel Quick Reference
Hard Disk Quick Reference
Harvard Graphics Quick Reference
MS-DOS Quick Reference
Microsoft Word Quick Reference
Norton Utilities Quick Reference
PC Tools Quick Reference, 2nd Edition
Q&A Quick Reference
QuickBASIC Quick Reference
Turbo Pascal Quick Reference
UNIX Programmer's Quick Reference
UNIX Shell Commands Quick Reference
Windows 3 Quick Reference
WordPerfect Quick Reference
WordPerfect 5.1 Quick Reference

Publishing Director

Lloyd J. Short

Series Product Director

Karen A. Bluestein

Senior Production Editor

Cheryl S. Robinson

Technical Editor

Gregory Croy

Proofreader

Betty Kish

Indexer

Jill Bomaster

Trademark Acknowledgments

Lotus 1-2-3 is a registered trademark of Ashton-Tate Corporation.

Microsoft Excel is a registered trademark of the Microsoft Corporation.

Table of Contents

Introduction

Microsoft Word 5.5 Quick Reference includes the quick reference information you need as you create, edit, format, and print Word documents, ranging from simple memos to complex funding proposals and legal briefs. Not a rehash of Microsoft's documentation, this book includes the most frequently used information from Que's best-selling publications on Microsoft Word 5.5.

Microsoft Word 5.5 Quick Reference is divided into sections by tasks, applications, and topics. Suppose that you want to center a heading and you cannot remember the procedure. Reach for this quick reference guide—you will find the information you want in the "Centering Text" section. Each section of this book contains step-by-step instructions for tasks Word 5.5 users undertake every day.

This book reviews Word 5.5 tasks, commands, and procedures, but it is not meant to take the place of a more comprehensive treatment of this extensive, flexible program. It assumes that you have installed Word successfully. This book does not attempt to teach you Word concepts; it is for review and reference.

If you are new to Word, and especially if you are new to personal computing, choose Que's *Using Microsoft Word 5.5: IBM Version.* Keep this quick reference guide next to your computer—and when you need help remembering how to carry out a task, reach for the step-by-step guidance you find on every page of this book.

HINTS FOR USING THIS BOOK

As you read this book, keep the following conventions in mind:

ASCII Files. The title of a section in this quick reference guide. For more information, turn to this section.

Window **C**lose. A Microsoft Word command name. To choose the command, type the boldfaced letters.

C:\MSWORD\LETTERS. Characters you type.

On-screen messages appear in a `special` typeface.

This guide assumes that you know how to choose Word commands and find your way through menus. If you need a further assistance, see Que's *Using Microsoft Word 5.5*.

COMMAND REFERENCE

The Command Reference includes an alphabetical listing of command tasks. Instructions for specific procedures appear under the appropriate task headings.

Accelerator Keys

Purpose

Enables you to select commands from drop-down menus or options within dialog boxes.

To use an accelerator key

Press and hold down the **Alt** key and then press the accelerator key.

Note

The accelerator key is the key that appears boldfaced.

Adding Text

Purpose

Enables you easily to add text to a document without disturbing existing text. Word 5.5 has two modes of operation: Insert and Overtype.

To toggle between the modes of operation

Press **Ins** to toggle between Insert mode and Overtype mode.

Notes

By default, Word operates in Insert mode. As you type, existing text moves forward and down automatically.

In Overtype mode, the characters you type erase existing text. When Word is in Overtype mode, the code `OT` appears on the status bar.

Anchoring a Paragraph

Purpose

Enables you to fix the position of a paragraph anywhere on the page so that it will remain there, even if you add more text above it.

To anchor a paragraph

1. Position the cursor within the paragraph or paragraphs you want to anchor.
2. Select Forma**T** P**O**sition (**Alt-TO**).

3. Select an option other than Inline in the **V**ertical list box.

   Options include Top, Centered, and Bottom.

4. If you want, select Pa**G**e in the Vertical area to position the text vertically measured from the top and bottom of the page.

5. Specify the horizontal position in the **H**orizontal list box if you do not want to use the flush left default setting.

6. To control how Word measures horizontal placement, select an option under “Relative to:” in the Horizontal area.

7. To increase or decrease the white space around the paragraph, type a measurement in the **D**istance from Text box.

   The default unit of measurement is inches.

8. If you are anchoring a graphic, drop down the Paragraph **W**idth list box and select Width of Graphic. If you are anchoring text, type a width to shorten or extend the default setting.

9. Select **OK**.

Note

An anchored paragraph is called a frame: a rectangular shape of fixed size and position. After you anchor the paragraph, the text you add to your document “floats” around the frame automatically. If there is room to the sides of the frame you have anchored, Word will automatically split the flow of text so that it flows past the frame to the left and right. You can place frames within multiple column text as well. When you use the Forma**T** P**O**sition command, you must specify how you want the frame anchored. To do so, specify a horizontal position and a vertical position. You also may control the amount of white space around the frame.

Annotating Text

Purpose

Enables you to add up to a 28-character reference mark to text. This feature is useful for collaborative writing.

To insert an annotation

1. Position the cursor where you want the annotation reference mark to appear.
2. Select **I**nsert **A**nnotation (**Alt-IA**).
3. Type an annotation reference mark up to 28 characters long.
4. Select Include **D**ate to insert the current date into the annotation text.
5. Select Include **T**ime to insert the current time into the annotation text.
6. Select **OK** to insert the annotation.
7. Type the text of the annotation.
8. Select **E**dit **G**o To (**Alt-EG**) to return to the document (at the annotation reference mark).

   Because the cursor was in the annotation you just typed, the Go To dialog box proposes the annotation number you just typed as the destination, and the Annotation option already is selected.
9. Select **OK**.

To edit an annotation

1. Select the reference mark of the annotation you want to edit.
2. Select **E**dit **G**o To (**Alt-EG**).

   or

   Use the **F5** keyboard shortcut.
3. Select **OK**.
4. Edit the annotation.

5. To return to the document at the annotation reference mark, select **E**dit **G**o To (**Alt-EG**).

   or

   Use the **F5** keyboard shortcut.

6. Select **OK**.

To move the cursor to the next annotation reference mark in a document

1. With the cursor positioned within the text of the document, select **E**dit **G**o To (**Alt-EG**).

   or

   Use the **F5** keyboard shortcut.

2. Select **A**nnotation.

3. Select **OK**.

To move an annotation

1. Highlight the annotation reference mark.

2. Select **E**dit Cu**T** (**Alt-ET**).

   or

   Use the **Shift-Del** keyboard shortcut.

3. Move the cursor to the place you want the annotation to appear.

4. Select **E**dit **P**aste (**Alt-EP**).

   or

   Use the **Shift-Ins** keyboard shortcut.

To merge annotations into one copy of a document

1. Select **F**ile **CL**ose All (**Alt-FL**) to close all document windows.

2. Select **M**acro **R**un (**Alt-MR**).

3. Highlight annot_merge and select **OK**.

   If you do not see the annot_merge in the list, select **M**acro **E**dit and open the MACRO.GLY glossary. Repeat Steps 2 and 3.

4. When you see the macro's dialog box, type a name for the document into which Word will collect the annotations.

5. When the macro asks whether you want to be prompted for the file names of the source documents, press **Y** and type the name of the first source file from which the macro copies annotations. Repeat the process for each source file. If you press **N**, the macro displays the **F**ile **M**anagement dialog box, which you can use to retrieve the source files.

To collect annotations

1. Turn off the **B**ackground Pagination option in the **U**tilities C**U**stomize dialog box before reviewing the copy of the document.

   Turning off **B**ackground Pagination ensures that reviewers' comments will not affect pagination.

2. Select **F**ile C**L**ose All (**Alt-FL**) to close all document windows.

3. Select **F**ile **N**ew (**Alt-FN**) to open a new, blank document.

4. Select **M**acro **R**un (**Alt-MR**).

5. Select annot_collect.

   If you do not see annot_collect, select Macro **E**dit and open the MACRO.GLY glossary. Repeat Steps 4 and 5.

6. Type the name of the file that will receive all the annotations.

   Choose a file name you have not used previously.

7. When the macro asks whether you want to be prompted for the file names of the source documents, press **Y** and type the name of the source file from which the macro copies the reviewer's annotations. If you press **N**, the macro displays the **F**ile Management dialog box, which you can use to retrieve the source files.

To remove all annotations from a document

1. Close all documents except the one from which you want to remove annotations.
2. Select **M**acro **R**un (**Alt-MR**).
3. Select annot_remove.

   If you do not see annot_remove, select Macro **E**dit and open the MACRO.GLY glossary. Repeat Steps 2 and 3.
4. After the macro runs, you are prompted to save the document using a new file name. Type a new file name and press **Enter**. The copy containing the annotations is preserved.

ASCII Files

Purpose

Enables you to save work as an ASCII text file, with hard carriage returns at the end of every line and no formatting codes.

To save a document as an ASCII file

1. Select **F**ile Save **A**s (**Alt-FA**).

   or

   Use the **Alt-F2** keyboard shortcut.
2. When the Save As dialog box appears, type a file name for the document in the File **N**ame text box.
3. Select Text Only w/Breaks from the Forma**T** list box.
4. Select **OK**.

Note

ASCII files often are required for telecommunications applications.

Backing Up

Purpose

Provides another copy of a document or file. Ensures the safekeeping of valuable data.

To copy files to a floppy disk

1. Select **F**ile **F**ile Management (**Alt-FF**).
2. Select the files you want to back up.

   You can select the files in the **F**iles list box. Place the highlight on the files and press the **Space bar** to mark the file.
3. Select **C**opy.
4. Use the **D**irectories window to select the drive or directory to which you want to copy the files.
5. Make sure that no X appears in the De**L**ete Files After Copy check box.
6. If you want to copy the document's style sheet, select Copy **S**tyle Sheets.
7. Select **OK**.

Notes

Perform regular backup routines. An excellent way to back up work for safekeeping is to copy new or altered files.

If Word finds a file on the destination disk with the same file name as the file you are copying, you see an alert box. To overwrite the file, select **OK**. To cancel the copying operation, select **Cancel**.

When you use DOS to copy many files at a time to a floppy disk, you may run out of room on the destination disk. DOS does not tell you which files remain uncopied. With File Management, you can see which files have been copied.

Blank Lines

Purpose

Enables you to insert blank lines in a document without disabling or limiting features.

To enter a blank line before each paragraph as you type

1. Select FormaT Paragraph (Alt-TP), and type 1 li in the Before text box.

   or

   Press Ctrl-O.

2. Type the text.

To return to the default format

1. Select FormaT Paragraph (Alt-TP).
2. Type 0 li in the Before text box.

To enter a blank line before each paragraph

1. Select the paragraphs.
2. Select FormaT Paragraph (Alt-TP).
3. Type 1 li in the Before text box.

   or

   Press Ctrl-O.

Note

Do not create blank lines in a document by pressing Enter. You may find later that this method forecloses some advanced options, such as automatic list sorting and the prevention of widowed headings.

Boilerplate Files

Purpose

Enables you to create and store on disk a document that contains text passages you use over and over.

To create boilerplate text using the glossary

1. Type the text. You can include character and paragraph formatting.
2. Select the text.
3. Select **E**dit Gl**O**ssary (**Alt-EO**).
4. In the **G**lossary Name text box, type a glossary name up to 31 characters long.
5. In the **O**ptional **K**eys text box, press the keys you want to use to enter the glossary at the cursor's location.
6. Select **D**efine.

To retrieve boilerplate text from the glossary

1. Type the glossary name in the document at the location where you want the boilerplate text to appear.
2. Press **F3**.

To create a boilerplate file using bookmarks

1. Open a new Word document.
2. Type a title for the first boilerplate passage.
3. After the title, on the same line, type **date** and press **F3** to enter the current date.
4. Press **Enter** and type the boilerplate passage. When you finish, press **Enter** again to separate the boilerplate passage from the text you want to place beneath it.
5. Select the first boilerplate passage.

6. Choose **I**nsert Book**M**ark (**Alt-IM**) and assign a bookmark name to the passage.
7. Repeat Steps 2 through 6 until you type and name all boilerplate passages.
8. Save the document.

To import boilerplate text from a bookmark file

1. Place the cursor where you want the imported text to appear.
2. Select **I**nsert **F**ile (**Alt-IF**).
3. Highlight the name of the boilerplate document in the Files list box.
4. Drop down the **R**ange list box.

   You see the list of bookmarks you created in the boilerplate document.
5. Select the bookmark you want to import.
6. Choose **L**ink to establish an active link between the two documents.

   By choosing this option, inserted text will be automatically updated when you make changes to the boilerplate text.
7. Select **OK**.

   Word inserts the bookmark text at the cursor's location.

Note

Above the bookmark text, Word inserts a coded line formatted as hidden text. Do not remove this line. Word needs this information to link and update the bookmark text. Because the line is formatted as hidden text, it does not print.

Bookmarks

Purpose

Enables you to mark sections of text so that you can jump immediately to a section of a lengthy document.

To mark text as a bookmark

1. Select the text you want to include in the bookmark.
2. Select **I**nsert Book**M**ark (**Alt-IM**).

   or

   Use the **Ctrl-Shift-F5** keyboard shortcut.
3. Type the bookmark name in the **B**ookmark Name text box.
4. Select **OK**.

To jump to a bookmark

1. Select **E**dit **G**o To.

   or

   Use the **F5** keyboard shortcut.
2. Select **B**ookmark.
3. Select the name of the bookmark in the Bookmark **N**ame list box.
4. Select **OK**.

To move bookmark text

1. Use **E**dit **G**o To to jump to the bookmark text.
2. You can use any selection technique to expand the highlight, but do not contract it.
3. Select **E**dit Cu**T**.

   or

   Press **Shift-Del** to cut the selection to the Scrap.
4. Move the cursor to the place you want the selection to appear.

5. Select **E**dit **P**aste.

   or

   Press **Shift-Ins** to paste the selection at the cursor's location.

To delete a bookmark

1. Select **I**nsert Book**M**ark (**Alt-IM**).
2. Highlight the name of the bookmark in the **B**ookmark Name list box.
3. Select **D**elete.
4. Select **OK**.

To change the text assigned to a bookmark name

1. Select the text.
2. Select **I**nsert Book**M**ark (**Alt-IM**).
3. In the **B**ookmark Names list box, select the name of the bookmark.
4. Select **OK**.

Notes

A bookmark's anchors are nonprinting characters. If you accidentally delete an anchor, Word assigns the anchor to the first character of the remaining bookmark text.

When you copy bookmark text within a document, Word copies the text, but not the bookmark.

Borders and Boxes

Purpose

Enables you to draw boxes around text and add shaded borders.

To add a single or double line beneath a heading

1. Select Forma**T** **B**order (**Alt-TB**).

2. Select **N**ormal line style to create a single line, or **D**ouble for a double line.

3. Select **L**ines.

4. Select **B**ottom.

5. Select **OK**.

To cancel a border and all other paragraph formats

1. Place the cursor in the paragraph containing the border you want to cancel.

2. Press **Ctrl-X**.

To cancel a border without canceling other paragraph formats

1. Place the cursor in the paragraph containing the border you want to cancel.

2. Select Forma**T** **B**orders (**Alt-TB**).

3. Select **N**one.

4. Select **OK**.

To shorten a border

1. Place the cursor in the paragraph containing the border you want to shorten.

2. Select Forma**T** **P**aragraph (**Alt-TP**).

3. Type an indent in the From Le**F**t or the From Ri**G**ht text box.

   You may type settings in both boxes to reduce the border from both sides of the margin.

4. Select **OK**.

To add lines or borders to a graphic

1. Place the cursor within the graphic's paragraph.

2. Select Forma**T** **B**orders (**Alt-TB**).

3. Select the line style you want to use.

   Line styles include Normal, Bold, Double, and Thick.

4. Select Box Each Paragraph to enclose the graphic in a box.

   Select Lines, and then choose Top, Bottom, Left, or Right to add lines.

5. Select **OK**.

Bulleted Lists

See *Indenting Text*.

Centering Text

Purpose

Enables you to position text in a document. You can center, justify, flush right, or flush left a paragraph.

To center a paragraph

1. Select Format Paragraph (**Alt-TP**).
2. Select the Center option button and select **OK**.

   or

   Use the **Ctrl-C** keyboard shortcut.

Character Formatting

Purpose

Enables you to attach special emphasis to characters, such as boldface or italic.

To select bold, italic, or underline with the mouse

1. Select View RiBbon to activate the Ribbon.

2. Select **Bld** (Bold), **Ital** (Italic), or **Ul** (Underline).

To select a character emphasis as you type or for the current selection

1. Select FormaT Character (**Alt-TC**).

2. Select the emphasis options you want, or use a keyboard shortcut.

To select boldface emphasis

Select Bold in the FormaT Character dialog box, or use the keyboard shortcut.

To select italic emphasis

Select Italic in the FormaT Character dialog box, or use the keyboard shortcut.

To select underline emphasis

Select Underline in the FormaT Character dialog box or use the keyboard shortcut.

To add character emphasis after you type

1. Select the text.

2. Select FormaT Character (**Alt-TC**) and choose a character format.

To cancel character formatting

You cancel character formatting by using any of the following methods:

- Select FormaT Character (**Alt-TC**) and turn off the format in the dialog box.

- Press the keyboard shortcut again to toggle off the format.

- Press **Ctrl-Z** to cancel position and emphasis choices, without canceling font, point size, or color choices.

- Press **Ctrl-Space bar** to cancel all formatting choices.

Keyboard Shortcuts

Format	*Shortcut*
Bold	**Ctrl-B**
Double Underline	**Ctrl-D**
Italic	**Ctrl-I**
Small Caps	**Ctrl-K**
Subscript	**Ctrl-=**
Superscript	**Ctrl-+** (or **Ctrl-Shift-=**)
Underline	**Ctrl-U**
Cancel formats	**Ctrl-Space bar**
Cancel formats without changing the current font and point size.	**Ctrl-Z**

Note

See also *Font, Hidden Text, Style Sheets,* and *Superscript and Subscript.*

Clearing the Screen

Purpose

Enables you to clear the screen of all distracting elements. You see nothing on-screen but the cursor, the end mark, and the text.

To display a clean screen

1. If the Ruler or Ribbon is displayed, select **V**iew **R**uler (**Alt-VR**) or **V**iew Ri**B**bon (**Alt-VB**) to turn off these features.

2. Select **V**iew **S**tatus Bar (**Alt-VS**) to turn off the display of the status bar.

3. Select **V**iew Pr**E**ferences (**Alt-VE**).
4. Select **M**enu (**Alt-M**), Window **B**orders (**Alt-B**), Messa**G**e Bar (**Alt-G**), **H**orizontal (**Alt-H**), and **V**ertical (**Alt-V**) until the X disappears from these check boxes.
5. Select **OK**.

Note

When you hide the window borders and scroll bars, you disable the mouse features that require the borders or bars. You must use the menus to perform actions such as closing, moving, and sizing windows, as well as turning on the Ruler and scrolling the screen.

Closing a Document

Purpose

Enables you to stop work on one document and continue working with a different document.

To close a document

Select **F**ile **C**lose (**Alt-FC**).

or

Click the close box in the upper left corner of the window.

Notes

If you have not saved changes you made to the document, you see an alert box. Select **Y**es to save the changes, **N**o to abandon them, or **Cancel** to leave the document on-screen.

See also *Quitting*.

Columns

Purpose

Enables you to produce multiple-column text. With this feature, you can create simple newsletters.

Side-by-Side Paragraphs

Side-by-side paragraphs are linked so that the paragraph printed on the left always is paired with the paragraph printed on the right. Price lists often contain side-by-side paragraphs because the text in one column must be linked with the text in the next column.

To create side-by-side paragraphs

1. In a new, blank Word document, press **Enter** to create a new, blank paragraph.
2. Place the cursor on the paragraph mark.
3. Select FormaT Paragraph (**Alt-TP**).
4. Type **3.25"** in the From RiGht text box, type **1 li** in the After box, and place an X in the Side by Side check box.
5. Select **OK**.
6. Press **Enter** to create a new paragraph.
7. Select FormaT Paragraph. Type **3.25"** in the From LeFt box, **0"** in the From RiGht box, and leave the other settings as they are.
8. Select **OK**.
9. To create additional side-by-side paragraphs, highlight both paragraph marks. Then select Edit Copy to copy the paragraph marks to the Scrap.
10. Position the cursor beneath the pair of paragraph marks.
11. Select Edit Paste or use the **Shift-Ins** shortcut to insert a copy of the pair of paragraph marks.
12. Repeat Step 11 to enter as many pairs as you need, up to a maximum of 16 pairs.

13. Type the text of the paragraphs.

To add an additional set of 16 pairs

1. After you create the 16th pair of side-by-side paragraphs, highlight both pairs.
2. Select FormaT Paragraph (**Alt-TP**).
3. Type **0 li** in the After box.
4. Select **OK**.
5. Place the cursor at the end of the last right paragraph and press **Enter**.
6. Select FormaT Paragraph (**Alt-TP**).
7. Remove the X from the Side by Side check box.
8. Select **OK**.
9. Highlight one of the pairs of side-by-side paragraphs, which are situated above the paragraph mark you just inserted.
10. Select Edit Copy or press **Ctrl-Ins** to copy the side-by-side paragraphs to the Scrap.
11. Place the cursor beneath the paragraph mark you inserted at the end of the side-by-side paragraphs.
12. Select Edit Paste or use the **Shift-Ins** keyboard shortcut to insert the side-by-side paragraphs at the cursor's location.
13. Delete the text of the paragraphs you just inserted, if any, but be careful not to delete the paragraph marks.
14. To create additional side-by-side paragraphs, highlight both paragraph marks. Then select Edit Copy or press **Ctrl-Ins** to copy the paragraph marks to the Scrap.
15. Position the cursor beneath the pair of paragraph marks.
16. Select Edit Paste or press **Shift-Ins** to insert a copy of the pair of paragraph marks.
17. Repeat Step 15 to enter as many pairs as you need, up to 16 pairs.

18. Type the text of the paragraphs.

To move the cursor from one column to the next in Layout View

Keys	*Moves the cursor to*
Ctrl-up arrow	Beginning of previous paragraph.
Ctrl-down arrow	Beginning of next paragraph.
Right arrow	Next column right.
Left arrow	Next column left.

Multiple-Column Text

Unlike side-by-side paragraphs, multiple columns have no relation to each other, except that one column begins where the preceding one left off.

To create multiple-column text

1. Place the cursor anywhere in the section you want to format with multiple columns.
2. Select FormaT Section (**Alt-TS**).
3. Type a number greater than 1 in the Number box of the Columns area.
4. If you want the columns separated by a space other than 0.5", type a different measurement in the Spacing box.
5. Select **OK**.

To add lines between columns

1. Place the cursor in the section containing multiple-column text.
2. Select FormaT Section (**Alt-TS**).
3. Type **0"** in the Spacing box.
4. Select **OK**.
5. Select all the paragraphs in the multiple-column section.

6. Select FormaT Borders (**Alt-TB**).
7. Select Lines, and when Word activates the check boxes below this option, select Left and Right.
8. Select **OK**.

To restore single-column formatting

1. Place the cursor anywhere in the section that contains unwanted multiple columns.
2. Select FormaT Section (**Alt-TS**).

   The Section dialog box is displayed.
3. Type **1** in the Number box of the Columns area.
4. Select **OK**.

To insert a manual column break

1. Position the cursor where you want the column break to occur.
2. Select Insert Break (**Alt-IB**) and select the Column option. Then select **OK**. Alternatively, use the **Ctrl-Shift-Enter** keyboard shortcut.

Notes

If all of the left paragraphs you are planning to type have just one line of text, don't bother with side-by-side paragraphs. Use hanging indents instead.

See also *Indenting Text* and *Headlines*.

Copying Files

See *Backing Up*.

Copying Text

Purpose

Enables you to copy text from one part of a document to another, from one document to a second document, or repeat text.

To copy text using the keyboard method

1. Select the text.
2. Select **E**dit **C**opy (**Alt-EC**) or use the **Ctrl-Ins** keyboard shortcut.
3. Move the cursor to the place you want the text to appear.
4. Select **E**dit **P**aste (**Alt-EP**) or use the **Shift-Ins** keyboard shortcut.

To copy text using the mouse method

1. Select the text you want to copy.
2. Move the pointer to the place you want the text to appear.
3. Press **Ctrl-Shift** and click the right mouse button.

To repeat the last text you typed

1. Press **Esc** twice to clear Edit Repeat's memory.
2. Type the text you want to copy.
3. Move the cursor to the new location and select **E**dit **R**epeat (**Alt-ER**) or use the **F4** keyboard shortcut.

Notes

You can continue to move the cursor to new locations and choose **E**dit **R**epeat to repeat the text throughout a document.

If you press **Enter**, type more text, or give a command, you clear the F4 memory.

Cross-Referencing

Purpose

Enables you to create an in-text reference to another part of the same document, items in a series, or footnote.

To cross-reference text

1. Select the text you want to cross-reference, and use **I**nsert Book**M**ark to define it as a bookmark.
2. Move the cursor to the place you want the text to appear.
3. Type the text of the cross-reference.

   For example, type **For a discussion of project methodology, see page** followed by a space.
4. Immediately following the cross-reference text, type the code name **page:** followed by the bookmark name. Do not type a space after the colon.
5. Press **F3**.

To mark a series item for cross-referencing

1. Place the cursor on the character preceding the series code name.
2. Select **I**nsert Book**M**ark (**Alt-IM**) or use the **Shift-Ctrl-F5** keyboard shortcut.
3. In the **B**ookmark Name text box, type a name for the bookmark that describes the contents of this specific item.
4. Select **OK**.

To cross-reference the series item

1. Position the cursor where you want the series item's number to appear.
2. Type the series code name, a colon, and the bookmark name, without any space.
3. Press **F3**.

To mark the footnote containing the full citation of a work

1. In the document, not in the footnote area, place the cursor on the space immediately following the footnote reference mark.
2. Select **I**nsert Book**M**ark (**Alt-IM**) or use the **Ctrl-Shift-F5** keyboard shortcut.
3. In the **B**ookmark Name, type the author's last name, an underscore character, and the date of publication.
4. Select **OK**.

To cross-reference the full citation of a work in a footnote

1. Insert the footnote and type the footnote text, including the text that immediately precedes the cross reference (such as See footnote n).
2. Type the code name **footnote:,** followed by the bookmark name you chose for the footnote containing the document's full citation. Do not include spaces.
3. Press **F3**.

Cursor-Movement Keys

Purpose

Equips you with a variety of keys for moving the cursor on-screen and scrolling up and down in a document.

Cursor-Movement Keys

Key	*Action*
Up arrow*	Moves cursor up one line.
Down arrow*	Moves cursor down one line.
Left arrow*	Moves cursor left one column.
Right arrow*	Moves cursor right one column.

Home	Moves cursor to the beginning of line.
End	Moves cursor to the end of line.
PgUp*	Moves cursor up one screen.
PgDn*	Moves cursor down one screen.
Ctrl-PgUp	Moves cursor to the top of screen.
Ctrl-PgDn	Moves cursor to the bottom of screen.
Ctrl-right arrow*	Moves cursor to next word.
Ctrl-left arrow*	Moves cursor to previous word.
Ctrl-up arrow*	Moves cursor to previous paragraph.
Ctrl-down arrow*	Moves cursor to next paragraph.
Ctrl-Home	Moves cursor to beginning of document.
Ctrl-End	Moves cursor to end of document.

*Key repeats action when held down.

Note

You cannot move the cursor past the end mark. If you try these cursor-movement techniques in a blank document, Word signals an error.

Deleting Files

Purpose

Enables you to delete files that you are sure you will never need again.

To delete files

1. Select **F**ile **F**ile Management (**Alt-FF**).
2. Select the files you want to delete.
3. Select **D**elete.
4. Select **OK**.

Note

If by mistake, you select a file you do not want to delete, select **Cancel** to abandon the delete operation.

Deleting Text

Purpose

Enables you to delete text you no longer need and to edit text.

To delete text permanently

Press **Backspace** to delete the character left of the cursor.

Press **Del** to delete the character on which the cursor is positioned.

To delete text to the Scrap

Select **E**dit Cu**T** (**Alt-ET**) or press **Shift-Del**.

Note

If you have used a previous version of Word, note that Del and Shift-Del have exchanged functions. Del does not route the text to the Scrap.

Dialog Box

Purpose

Conveys an on-screen message or requests information.

To move around in a dialog box

To move from one area to another within a dialog box, press **Tab**.

To move in the opposite direction, press **Shift-Tab**.

To activate an area, press and hold down the **Alt** key and press the accelerator key.

To display a drop-down list box

1. Activate the area.
2. Press **Alt-down arrow**.

   or

   If you are using a mouse, click the down-arrow symbol next to the list box.

   Close a drop-down list box by pressing **Alt-down arrow** again.

To select a check box item

Press **Alt** and the box's accelerator key.

or

If you are using a mouse, click the box.

To select an option button

Press **Alt** and the button's accelerator key.

or

If you are using a mouse, click the button.

To select a command button

Press **Tab** to highlight the button and then press **Enter**.

or

If you are using a mouse, click the button.

DOS

Purpose

Enables you to access DOS at any time you use Word 5.5.

To access DOS

1. Select **F**ile **S**ave (**Alt-FS**) to save the document or **F**ile Sav**E** All (**Alt-FE**) if you are working with more than one document.
2. Select **F**ile **D**OS Commands (**Alt-FD**).
3. Type the DOS command.
4. Select **OK**.
5. When the command is finished executing, press any key to return to Word.

Exiting Word

See *Quitting*.

File Management

Purpose

Enables you to perform essential file maintenance tasks and gives you powerful tools to search the contents of an entire hard disk.

To change the default search path

1. Select **F**ile **F**ile Management (**Alt-FF**).
2. Select **S**earch.

3. Activate the **D**irectories list box, and use the arrow keys to highlight a directory that contains Word documents.
4. Press the comma (**,**) key.
5. Repeat Steps 3 and 4 until you have added all the directories that may contain Word documents.
6. Select **OK**.

To choose a sort option

1. Select Op**T**ions.
2. In the area titled Sort Files By, select one of the option buttons.
3. Select **OK**.

To change the view

1. Select Op**T**ions.
2. In the area titled View Files, select **S**hort, **L**ong, or **F**ull.
3. Select **OK**.

To move files to a floppy disk

1. Select the files you want to move.
2. Select **C**opy.
3. Select the De**L**ete Files After Copy check box so that you see an X.
4. Use the **D**irectories window to select the drive or directory to which you want to move the files.
5. Select **OK**.

To reduce the number of files displayed in the Files list

1. In the File Management dialog box, select **S**earch.
2. Type the search criteria in one of the text boxes.
3. Repeat Step 2 for other text boxes.
4. Select **M**atch Case to match the exact pattern of upper- and lowercase letters, if you want.

5. Select **OK**.

To restore the display of all Word files

1. Select Search.
2. Delete all the text in the Search dialog box's text boxes, except Search Paths.
3. Select **OK**.

To rename a file

1. Select File File Management (**Alt-FF**).
2. Place the highlight bar on the file you want to rename.
3. Select ReName.
4. Type the new file name.
5. Select **OK**.

Notes

Within text Search boxes, you can formulate expressions using the following logical operators:

Operator	*Result*
Smith, Jones	Retrieves documents written by Smith, also retrieves documents written by Jones.
Smith~Jones	Retrieves documents written by Smith, but not those written by Jones.
Smith&Jones	Retrieves documents only if they were jointly written by Smith and Jones.
>9/21/90	Retrieves documents created after 9/21/90.
<9/21/90	Retrieves documents created before 9/21/90.

Word evaluates any expression containing logical operators by reading the NOT operator first, followed by the AND operator and the OR operator. You can change the order of evaluation by enclosing the expression in parentheses.

Font

Purpose

Enables you to select from the available character sets you have installed on your system.

To change the font as you type or for the current selection

1. Select FormaT Character (Alt-TC).
2. Drop down the Font list box.

   You see a list of the font choices available for your printer.
3. Select the font.
4. Select OK.

To select a nondefault font for an entire document

1. Press Ctrl-5 (on the numeric keypad) to select the entire document.
2. Select FormaT Character (Alt-TC).
3. Drop down the Font list box.

   You see a list of the font choices available for your printer.
4. Select a font.
5. Select OK.

Footnote

Purpose

Enables you to add text at the bottom of a page as a reference.

To insert a footnote

1. Position the cursor where you want the footnote reference mark to appear.
2. Select **I**nsert Foot**N**ote (**Alt-IN**).
3. Type a footnote reference mark up to 28 characters long.

   or

   Leave the X in the **A**uto-numbered Reference if you want Word to number the note automatically.
4. Select **OK**.
5. Type the text of the footnote.
6. Select **E**dit **G**o To (**Alt-EG**).
7. Select **OK**.
8. If you want the reference mark to appear as a superscript, press **Ctrl-+**.

To determine footnote placement

1. Place the cursor in the section that contains the footnotes you want to affect.
2. Select Forma**T** **S**ection (**Alt-TS**).
3. Select S**A**me Page to place the notes at the bottom of the page, or choose En**D** of Section to place the notes at the end of the section.
4. Select **OK**.

To edit a footnote

1. Select the reference mark of the note you want to edit.
2. Select **E**dit **G**o To (**Alt-EG**) or use the **F5** keyboard shortcut.

3. Select **OK**.
4. Edit the note.
5. Select **E**dit **G**o To (**Alt-EG**) or use the **F5** keyboard shortcut.
6. Select **OK**.

To move the cursor to the next footnote reference mark

1. Select **E**dit **G**o To (**Alt-EG**) or use the **F5** keyboard shortcut.
2. Select **F**ootnote.
3. Select **OK**.

To delete a footnote

1. Position the cursor on the footnote reference mark.
2. Press **Del**.

To move a footnote

1. Highlight the footnote reference mark.
2. Select **E**dit Cu**T** (**Alt-ET**) or use the **Shift-Del** keyboard shortcut.
3. Move the cursor to the place you want the note to appear.
4. Select **E**dit **P**aste (**Alt-EP**) or use the **Shift-Ins** keyboard shortcut.

To format footnotes after you type them

1. Press **Ctrl-Home** to move the cursor to the first character in a document.
2. Select **E**dit **G**o To (**Alt-EG**) or press the **F5** keyboard shortcut.
3. Select **F**ootnote.
4. Select **OK**.

   Word jumps to the first footnote reference mark.
5. Select **E**dit **G**o To (**Alt-EG**).
6. Use any selection technique to expand the highlight until you highlight all the footnotes.

7. Use character and formatting commands to format all the notes at once.

To see the text of footnotes with reference marks currently displayed in the document window

Select **V**iew **F**ootnotes/Annotations (**Alt-VF**).

Press **F6** to see the next pane.

Note

The position of notes is a section format, controlled by the Section dialog box. The footnote numbers that Word inserts are also a section format. When Word comes to a new division, the program restarts footnote numbers at 1.

Form Letters

Purpose

Enables you to create a letter that is sent to many people but personalized so that the letter appears as if it is sent only to one person.

Creating the Data Document

A data document contains the information you want Word to insert into a form letter. The data document consists of the header record and the main document. The header record lists the field names you plan to use in the form letter. The main document is the text you want to print on every copy of the form letter.

To create a header record

1. Open a new, blank document.
2. Type the header record, separating each field name with a comma or tab keystroke.

   For example, a typical header looks like this:

LASTNAME,FIRSTNAME,SALUTATION, COMPANY_NAME, STREET_ADDRESS, CITY, STATE, ZIP

3. At the end of the line, press **Enter**.
4. Type the first data record, entering the data in the order established in the data record. Be sure to use exactly the same number of tabs or commas you used in the header record. A typical data record follows:

   Williams, Nancy, Dr.,University of Western Maryland, 210H Jacobs Hall,College City,MD,20298

5. Press **Enter** to start a new line.
6. Repeat Steps 4 and 5 until you have typed all the data records. Do not press Enter at the end of the last record.
7. Save the document.

To create the main document

1. Type a DATA instruction on the first line. Press **Ctrl-[** to enter the left chevron. Type the word **DATA** followed by a space, and then type the name of the data document.

   You can omit the period and DOC extension. Press **Ctrl-]** to close the DATA instruction.

2. Press **Enter**.
3. Type the text that you want to print on every copy of the document.
4. Insert field names into the document where you want Word to insert data from the data document. To type a field name, press **Ctrl-[** to enter the left chevron. Type the exact field name. Press **Ctrl-]** to enter the right chevron.
5. Save the main document.

To use data drawn from a database management program

1. Print the data to an ASCII file, separated by commas or tabs.

2. Open the ASCII file with Word.
3. Add a header record at the beginning of the document. You must add one field name for each data field in the data records below.
4. Check to make sure that each data record has exactly the same number of fields.
5. Save the document.

Sorting and Renumbering Data

The sorting techniques are useful for putting a data document in order, alphabetized by last name.

To sort and renumber the data document

1. Open the data document.

   Note that data must be arranged in column form to make sorting possible.
2. Select FormaT Margins (**Alt-TM**).
3. Type a measurement in the Width text box that will allow the longest record to fit on one line.
4. Select **OK**.
5. Create columns by setting tab stops for each field.
6. Press **Tab** to place the fields in the proper column.
7. Position the cursor at the upper right corner of the column you want to use as the sort key.
8. Press **Ctrl-Shift-F8** to toggle on the Column-select mode.
9. Select the entire column, but do not select the header record.
10. Select Utilities SOrt (**Alt-UO**).
11. Select Ascending sort order and, in the key type area, ALphanumeric.
12. Select **OK**.

Printing

You can choose to print all records or only those you specify.

To print the Merge application

1. Open the main document.
2. Select **F**ile Print **M**erge (**Alt-FM**).
3. Select **P**rint.
4. Select **OK**.

To print to a Word file

1. Open the main document.
2. Select **F**ile Print **M**erge (**Alt-FM**).
3. Select **N**ew Document.
4. Type a name for the document.
5. Select **OK**.

To print records you specify

1. Open the main document.
2. Select **F**ile Print **M**erge (**Alt-FM**).
3. Select **R**ecords.

   In the Records box, type the numbers of the data records you want to print. You can type individual numbers (**1,3,9**), a series (**9-27**), or a combination of the two (**1,3,9-27**).
4. Select **P**rint.
5. Select **OK**.

Mailing Labels

Word can print these labels from the mailing list you already created. Depending on your printer's capabilities, you can print addresses on continuous-feed labels and sheet-feed labels.

To print continuous-feed labels

1. Open a new, blank document.
2. On the first line of the document, type a DATA instruction to tell Word where to find the data.
3. Type the first line of field names on the same line as the DATA instruction, with no space between the DATA instruction and the first field name.
4. Press **Enter** to start a new line.
5. Type the second line of field names you want printed on the mailing labels.
6. Press **Enter** to start a new line.
7. Type the third line of field names you want printed on the mailing labels.
8. Select FormaT Margins (**Alt-TM**).
9. In the Height text box, type the height of the labels you are using.
10. In the Top, Bottom, and Right text boxes, type **0"**.
11. In the Left text box, type an indentation (such as **0.25"** or **0.5"**) so that Word will not start printing at the left edge of the labels.
12. Select **OK**.
13. Select File Print Merge (**Alt-FM**).
14. Select Print.
15. Select **OK**.

To print single-column sheet-fed labels

1. Open a new, blank document.
2. Select View PrEferences (**Alt-VE**), and make sure that an X appears in the Paragraph Marks check box.
3. On the first line of the document, type a DATA instruction to tell Word where to find the data.
4. Type the first line of field names on the same line as the DATA instruction, with no spaces between the DATA instruction and the first field name.

5. Press **Enter** to start a new line.
6. Type the second line of field names you want printed on the mailing labels.
7. Press **Enter** to start a new line.
8. Type the third line of field names you want printed on the mailing labels.
9. Press **Enter** twice.
10. Type **<<NEXT>>**, and without pressing Enter, type the first line of field names on the same line as the NEXT instruction with no space between the DATA instruction and the first field name.
11. Type the rest of the field labels, and press **Enter** twice.
12. Select the second set of data fields. Be sure to include the NEXT instruction and the two trailing paragraph marks.
13. Select **E**dit **C**opy (**Alt-EC**) or press **Ctrl-Ins**.
14. Place the cursor on the last paragraph mark in the document and press **Enter**.
15. Select **E**dit **P**aste (**Alt-EP**) or press **Shift-Ins** to paste copies of the data fields in the document.
16. Make sure that exactly two blank lines appear between each set of data fields.
17. Select Forma**T** **M**argins (**Alt-TM**).
18. In the **H**eight text box, type the height of the labels you are using.
19. In the **T**op, **B**ottom, and **R**ight text boxes, type **0"**.
20. In the **L**eft text box, type an indentation (such as **0.25"** or **0.5"**) so that word will not start printing at the left edge of the labels. If you are using a laser printer, try a **0.25"** top margin and a **0.5"** bottom margin.
21. Select **OK**.
22. Select **F**ile Print **M**erge (**Alt-FM**).

23. Select Print.

24. Select **OK**.

To print three-column sheet-fed labels

1. Follow Steps 1 through 13 in the preceding set of instructions (on printing single-column sheet-fed labels).

2. Select Edit Paste (**Alt-EP**) or press **Shift-Ins** to paste copies of the data fields in the document.

3. Make sure that exactly three blank lines appear between each set of data fields.

4. Select FormaT Section (**Alt-TS**).

5. Type **3** in the Number text box.

6. Type **0"** in the Spacing text box.

7. Select Column in the SEction Start drop-down list box.

8. Select Margins.

9. In the Height text box, type the height of the labels you are using.

10. In the Top, Bottom, and Right text boxes, type **0"**.

11. In the Left text box, type an indentation (such as **0.25"** or **0.5"**) so that Word will not start printing at the left edge of the labels.

12. Select **OK**.

13. Select File Print Merge (**Alt-FM**).

14. Select Print.

15. Select **OK**.

Formats

Purpose

Enables you to to select the values for such settings as character emphasis, font, line height, measurement, paragraphs, tabs, and type size.

Default Formats

Word 5.5 has the following default character and paragraph formats:

Format	*Setting*
Character emphasis	None
Font	Printer's standard (such as Pica or Courier)
Line height	12 points (6 lines to an inch)
Measurement	Inches
Paragraphs	Single-spaced, flush-left alignment
Tabs	Every 0.5 inch
Type size	12-point height, 10 character per inch (10 pitch)

Working with Formats

To copy a format with a mouse

1. Select the characters you want to format.
2. Point to a character or paragraph that already contains the format you want to use.
3. Hold down the **Ctrl** and **Shift** keys and click the left mouse button.

To repeat a single format

1. Select the first instance of the text you want to format.
2. Select the character or paragraph formatting command.
3. Select the next instance of the text you want to format the same way.
4. Select **E**dit **R**epeat (**Alt-ER**) or use the **F4** keyboard shortcut.

To replace formats throughout an entire document

1. Press **Ctrl-Home** to position the cursor at the beginning of the document.
2. Select **E**dit R**E**place (**Alt-EE**).
3. In the Replace dialog box, select Replace **F**ormatting Only.
4. Select **C**haracter or **P**aragraph.
5. Select the format or formats you want Word to remove.
6. Select **R**eplace With.
7. Select the format or formats you want Word to place in the document.
8. Select **OK**.
9. Click **X** to change Replace Selection to Replace All, and then click **Y**.

To search for formats

1. Press **Ctrl-Home** to position the cursor at the beginning of the document.
2. Select **E**dit **S**earch.
3. In the Search dialog box, select Search for **F**ormatting Only.
4. Select **C**haracter or **P**aragraph.
5. Select the format or formats for which you want to search.

6. Select **OK**.
7. To repeat the search, press **Shift-F4**.

Forms

Purpose

Enables you to design a business form that provides precisely the information needed to accomplish a specific task. With Word 5.5, you can set up the form on-screen and then have it reproduced for use. Or, you can supply the information on-screen.

To add a data entry mark to a form so that the user knows where to enter data

1. Position the cursor where you want the data entry mark to appear.
2. Press **Ctrl-]**.
3. Format the data entry mark as hidden text.

To move the cursor to data entry marks

Press **Ctrl->** (greater than) to move to the next data entry mark.

Press **Ctrl-<** (less than) to move to the previous data entry mark.

To create a form that prompts the user to supply the needed information

1. At the top of the form you created, press **Ctrl-[** to enter a left chevron.
2. Type **ASK** followed by a field name, an equal sign, and a question mark.

   For example, type

   ASK,lastname = ?

   If you want Word to display a message on-screen when it prompts the user to supply the needed data, type the message after the question mark.

3. Press **Ctrl-]** to close the ASK statement.
4. Place the cursor where you want Word to print the information the user will supply.
5. Press **Ctrl-[** to enter a left chevron.
6. Type the same field name you used in the ASK statement.
7. Press **Ctrl-]** to enter a right chevron.
8. Repeat Steps 1 through 7 until you have written all ASK statements and entered field names for all information you want the user to supply.
9. Format the ASK statements as hidden text.

To print a form that includes ASK statements

1. Select **F**ile Print **M**erge (**Alt-FM**).
2. Select **P**rint.
3. Select **OK**.

Glossary

Purpose

Enables you to store text and macros.

Entering a Glossary

To create a glossary entry

1. Type the text you want the entry to contain. You can include character and paragraph formatting.
2. Select the text.
3. Select **E**dit Gl**O**ssary (**Alt-EO**).
4. In the **G**lossary Name text box, type a glossary name up to 31 characters long.
5. In the Optional **K**eys area, press the keys you want to use to enter the glossary entry at the cursor's location.

6. Select **D**efine.

To retrieve a glossary entry when you know its name

1. Type the glossary name in the document.
2. Press **F3**.

To retrieve a glossary entry from the Glossary dialog box

1. Select **E**dit Gl**O**ssary (**Alt-EO**).

   You see the Glossary dialog box.

2. Select the **N**ames area and highlight the glossary name.
3. Select **I**nsert.

To edit a glossary entry

1. Insert the entry.
2. Edit the text.
3. Select the text.
4. Select **E**dit Gl**O**ssary (**Alt-EO**).
5. Highlight the glossary entry's name in the Names list box.
6. Select **D**efine.
7. Select **OK** to replace the glossary entry.

To add a keyboard shortcut to an often-used glossary entry

1. Insert the entry.
2. Select the text.
3. Select **E**dit Gl**O**ssary (**Alt-EO**).
4. Highlight the glossary entry's name in the Names list box.
5. Select the Optional **K**eys area.
6. Press the key combination you want to use.
7. Select **D**efine.
8. Select **OK** to replace the glossary entry.

To delete a glossary entry

1. Select Edit GlOssary (**Alt-EO**).
2. Highlight the glossary entry's name in the Names list box.
3. Select DeLete.
4. Press **Esc** to return to the document.

Supplied Glossary Entries

To enter the current time or date

1. Place the cursor where you want the time or date to appear.
2. Type **time** or **date**.
3. Press **F3**.

To enter the time or date at the time of printing

1. Place the cursor where you want the time or date to appear when your document is printed.
2. Type **timeprint** or **dateprint**.
3. Press **F3**.

Glossary Files

To abandon the glossary entries you created in a session

1. Exit Word without saving the current glossary.
2. When you see the alert box informing you that you have not saved the glossary, select No to abandon the entries you created.

To clear all glossaries you created and saved in a glossary file

1. Select Edit GlOssary (**Alt-EO**).
2. Select Clear All.
3. Select Yes to confirm the action.
4. Select Edit GlOssary (**Alt-EO**).

5. Select **S**ave Glossary.

6. Select **OK**.

To save the current glossary entries to NORMAL.GLY

1. Select **E**dit Gl**O**ssary (**Alt-EO**).

2. Select **S**ave Glossary.

3. Select **OK**.

To save the entries in a new glossary file

1. Select **E**dit Gl**O**ssary (**Alt-EO**).

2. Select **S**ave Glossary.

3. Type a file name for the glossary file.

4. Select **OK**.

To load a glossary file other than NORMAL.GLY

1. Select **E**dit Gl**O**ssary (**Alt-EO**).

2. Select **O**pen Glossary.

3. If you see the glossary file name in the **F**iles list box, highlight the name. If not, use the Directories list box to find the file in another directory.

4. Select **OK**.

To merge two glossary files

1. Select **E**dit Gl**O**ssary (**Alt-EO**).

2. Select **O**pen Glossary and open the first glossary file.

3. Select Me**R**ge.

4. If you see the glossary file name in the **F**iles list box, highlight the name. If not, use the **D**irectories list box to find the file in another directory.

5. Select **OK**.

6. If you want to save the merged glossaries, select **S**ave Glossary.

To print the current glossary

1. Select **F**ile **P**rint (**Alt-FP**) or use the **Shift-F9** keyboard shortcut.
2. Drop down the **P**rint list box.
3. Select Glossary.
4. Close the Print list box.
5. Select **OK**.

Note

See also *Boilerplate Files*.

Graphics

Purpose

Enables you to incorporate graphics, such as graphs generated by spreadsheet programs, into document files. You can size, move, and enclose the graphics in boxes or add lines. You also can anchor the graphic image to any paragraph.

To insert a picture at the cursor's location

1. If you see the code `LY` on the status bar, select **V**iew **L**ayout (**Alt-VL**) to toggle the layout view off.
2. Place the cursor where you want the image to appear.
3. Select **I**nsert **P**icture (**Alt-IP**).
4. Highlight the graphic's file name in the **F**iles list box.
5. Select **P**review to import the image and to see how the page will look with the graphic imported into the cursor's location. Alternatively, select **OK** to import the image without previewing.

To size and position a graphic after importing

1. Highlight the hidden text code that Word inserted when you imported the graphic.

2. Select **I**nsert **P**icture (**Alt-IP**).
3. To change the alignment of the image in its frame, select an option from the A**L**ign in Frame list box.
4. To change the width of the graphic, type a measurement in the **W**idth list box.
5. You can override the automatically-computed height by typing a measurement in the **H**eight list box.
6. To add space before or after the graphic, type measurements in the **B**efore and **A**fter text boxes.
7. Select **OK**.

To add lines or borders to a graphic

1. Position the cursor within the graphic's paragraph.
2. Select Forma**T** **B**orders (**Alt-TB**).
3. Select a line style, if you want a style other than the Nor**M**al default.
4. Select **B**ox Each Paragraph to enclose the graphic in a box.
5. Select **L**ines, and select Top, Bottom, Left, and Right to add lines.
6. Select **OK**.

To add a caption

1. Position the cursor on the paragraph mark that ends the information about the graphic, and press **Shift-Enter** to start a new line. Press **Shift-Enter** again.
2. Type the caption.
3. Press **Ctrl-C** to center the caption. Preview the caption with Print Preview.

To change the graphics resolution

1. Select **F**ile **P**rint (**Alt-FP**).
2. Select **O**ptions.
3. Select **G**raphics Resolution and drop down the list box.

4. Select the resolution you want from the list box.
5. Select **OK** to confirm your choices in the Print Options menu.

Notes

Many graphics programs permit you to save files in one of the formats Word can read. For example, you can save a Harvard Graphics chart in PCX, EPS, or HPGL format.

See also *Anchoring a Paragraph.*

Gutter

Purpose

Adds extra white space to the inside margin, the one that is next to the binding.

To add a gutter to a document

1. Select FormaT Margins (**Alt-TM**).

   You see the Section Margins dialog box.

2. Type the gutter width in the Gutter text box.
3. Select **OK**.

Notes

If you are binding a document that you plan to print or photocopy on one side of the page only, you do not need a gutter; you just add extra width to the left margin.

When you type a gutter measurement in the Gutter text box, Word assumes that you are going to photocopy the document on both sides of the page. Word adds the measurement to the inside margin, that is, to the right side of even-numbered pages and to the left side of odd-numbered pages.

Headers and Footers

Purpose

Enables you to create running heads and headers at the top margin of a document. Footers appear within the bottom margin. Headers and footers frequently include text that identifies the document.

To add a header or footer to a document

1. Place the cursor at the beginning of the section in which you want the header or footer to appear.
2. Type the header or footer text and format the text.
3. Make sure that the header or footer text is separated from the rest of the document's text by a paragraph break. If it is not, position the cursor at the end of the last line of the header or footer and press **Enter**.
4. Select the header or footer paragraphs.
5. If you see the code `LY` at the bottom of the screen, select **V**iew **L**ayout to toggle the layout view off.
6. Select Forma**T** **H**eader/Footer (**Alt-TH**).
7. In the Format As area, select the **H**eader or **F**ooter option.
8. In the Print On area, select First **P**age to turn on headers or footers on page one. You also may remove the `X` from O**D**d Pages if you want to suppress the header or footer on these pages.
9. Select **OK**.

To add page numbers to an existing header or footer

1. Within the header or footer text, place the cursor where you want the page number to appear.
2. Type **page**.
3. Press **F3**.

To create headers or footers for two-sided documents

1. Place the cursor at the beginning of the section in which you want the header or footer to appear.
2. Type the text for the odd pages' header or footer. Add page numbers and formatting.
3. Press **Enter**.
4. Type the text for the even pages' header or footer. Add page numbers and formatting.
5. Select the first header or footer paragraph (the one to be printed on odd pages).
6. If you see the code LY at the bottom of the screen, select **V**iew **L**ayout to toggle the layout view off.
7. Select Forma**T** **H**eader/Footer (**Alt-TH**).
8. In the Format As area, select the **H**eader or **F**ooter option.
9. Select **E**ven pages so that the X disappears from the check box. Only the O**D**d Pages options should remain checked.
10. Select **OK**.
11. Select the second header or footer paragraph.
12. Select Forma**T** **H**eader/Footer (**Alt-TH**).
13. In the Format As area, select the **H**eader or **F**ooter option.
14. Select O**D**d Pages so that the X disappears from the check box. Only the **E**ven Pages options should remain checked.
15. Select **OK**.

To display header and footer codes

1. Select **V**iew Pr**E**ferences (**Alt-VE**).
2. Select St**Y**le Bar in the Show area so that an X appears next to the option.
3. Select **OK**.

To reposition the header or footer text vertically

1. Select the header or footer.
2. Select FormaT Header/Footer (**Alt-TH**).
3. Select Options.

   You see the Header/Footer Options dialog box.
4. Type a new vertical position in the Header Position from Top or Footer Position from Bottom text boxes.
5. Select **OK**.

To delete a header or footer

1. Select the header or footer paragraph, including its paragraph mark.
2. Press **Del**.

To continue a header or footer with new text

1. Place the cursor just above the page break of the page where you want the change to occur.
2. Type the new text.
3. Select FormaT Header (**Alt-TH**).
4. Select exactly the options in the Header/Footer dialog box that you used for the first version of the header.
5. Select **OK**.

To add page numbers

1. Select Insert Page-NUmbers (**Alt-IU**).
2. Turn page numbers on by choosing From Top (for page numbers at the top of the page) or From Bottom (for page numbers at the bottom of the page).
3. To change the vertical placement of the page number from the top or bottom, enter a new measurement in the text box next to From Top or From Bottom.
4. To change the horizontal alignment of the page number, select an option in the Align Page Number At area.

5. If you want, select a new page number format from the **F**ormat drop-down list box.
6. To start page numbering with a number other than 1, type the number in the **S**tart At text box.

   The default option, Auto, starts page numbering at 1.
7. Select **OK**.

To create a header or footer that contains page numbers only

1. Place the cursor at the beginning of the section in which you want the header or footer to appear.
2. Type **page**.
3. Press **F3**.
4. If you want to format the page numbers, select (page) and use the Forma**T** **C**haracter or Forma**T** **P**aragraph command.
5. Make sure that the header or footer text is separated from the rest of the document's text by a paragraph break. If it isn't, position the cursor at the end of the last character of the header or footer and press **Enter**.
6. Select the header or footer paragraphs.
7. If you see the code `LY` at the bottom of the screen, select **V**iew **L**ayout to toggle the layout view off.
8. Select Forma**T** **H**eader/Footer (**Alt-TH**).

To add page numbers in the "Page X of Total" format

1. Press **Ctrl-End** to move the cursor to the end of the document.
2. Select the last word in the document.
3. Select **I**nsert Book**M**ark (**Alt-IM**).
4. Type **lastpage** in the **B**ookmark Name text box.

5. Select **OK**.
6. Press **Ctrl-Home** to move the cursor to the top of the document.
7. Type **Page page** and press **F3**.
8. On the same line, type a space and then type **of page:lastpage**.
9. Press **F3**.
10. Press **Enter** to separate this text from the rest of the document.
11. Select the header or footer text, and select Forma**T** **H**eader/Footer (**Alt-TH**) to mark the text as header or footer text.

To control the page number format for page numbers entered in headers or footers

1. Place the cursor within the section containing the `(page)` symbol you want to affect.
2. Select **I**nsert Page N**U**mbers (**Alt-IU**).
3. Select a page number format from the **F**ormat drop-down list box.
4. Select **OK**.

To start page numbers at a number other than 1 for page numbers entered in headers or footers

1. Place the cursor within the section containing the `(page)` symbol you want to affect.
2. Select **I**nsert Page N**U**mbers (**Alt-IU**).
3. Type the number in the **S**tart At text box.
4. Select **OK**.

Headlines

Purpose

Enables you to add a heading to a document.

To add a single-column headline in a multiple-column document

1. Press **Ctrl-Home** to place the cursor at the beginning of the document.
2. Select FormaT Section (**Alt-TS**).
3. Select Continuous from the SEction Start list box.
4. Select **OK**.
5. Select Insert Break (**Alt-IB**).
6. Select Section.
7. Select **OK**.
8. Press **Ctrl-Home** again to place the cursor before the section mark.
9. Select FormaT Section (**Alt-TS**).
10. Type **1** in the Number box.
11. Select **OK**.
12. Type the headline.

Help

Purpose

Provides on-screen help about Word 5.5. You can obtain Help in two ways. To obtain context-sensitive Help, press **F1** to display a screen of information about the command or feature that is currently highlighted. To view the Help Index, which provides access to the keyboard maps, Word 5.5 upgrade information, definitions, and procedures, select Help.

To obtain context-sensitive Help at any time

1. Highlight the command name or dialog box area for which you want help.
2. Press **F1**.
3. Press **PgDn** or select the Page **D**n command button to display the next page, if one is available.

To obtain an on-screen list of instructions for common Word procedures

1. Select **H**elp **I**ndex (**Alt-HI**).
2. Select the **P**rocedure command button.
3. Select the procedure you want from the alphabetical list. If necessary, use **PgUp**, **PgDn**, or scroll with the mouse to see additional pages of the Procedure Index.
4. Select Exit to return to the document.

To display definitions of key terms

1. Select **H**elp **I**ndex (**Alt-HI**).
2. Select the Definitions command button.
3. Select the term you want from the alphabetical list. If necessary, use **PgUp**, **PgDn**, or scroll with the mouse to see additional pages of the Procedure Index.
4. Select **OK** to return to the terms list.
5. Select Exit to return to the document.

To view help screens about the keyboard

1. Select **H**elp **I**ndex (**Alt-HI**).
2. Select the Mouse command button.
3. Select Exit to quit Help.
4. Select a topic from the Mouse menu.
5. Select Exit to return to the document.

To view help screens about display screen regions

1. Select **H**elp **I**ndex (**Alt-HI**).

2. Select the Screen Regions command button.
3. Point to the region of the screen you want to explore and click the left mouse button. Alternatively, use the arrow keys to place the cursor in the region and press **Enter**.
4. Click **OK** to return to the screen region display.
5. Repeat Steps 3 and 4 for additional screen regions.
6. Select Exit to return to the document.

To view help screens about learning Word 5.5 for Word 5.0 users

1. Select **H**elp Word **5**.0 to 5.5 (**Alt-H5**).
2. Select a topic from the Word 5.0 to 5.5 menu.
3. Select Exit to return to the document.

Hidden Text

Purpose

Enables you to embed comments in a document so that they do not appear on the printed work.

To create hidden text as you type

1. If you see the `LY` code on the status line, select **V**iew **L**ayout to turn the View Layout mode off.

   You cannot see hidden text in the View Layout mode, and because you are creating the text as you format, you must be able to see what you are doing.

2. Select **V**iew Pr**E**ferences and see whether the H**I**dden Text check box contains an `X`. If it doesn't, select H**I**dden Text.
3. Select **OK**.
4. Select Forma**T** **C**haracter (**Alt-TC**) and select the **H**idden check box so that you place an `X` in the check box. Next, choose **OK**. Alternatively, use the **Ctrl-H** keyboard shortcut.

5. Type the text you want to hide.

6. Select FormaT Character (**Alt-TC**) and select the **H**idden Text check box again to remove the X. Next, select **OK**. Alternatively, use the **Ctrl-H** keyboard shortcut again.

To create hidden text after you type

1. Select the text.

2. Select FormaT Character (**Alt-TC**) and select the **H**idden check box so that you place an X in the check box. Next, choose **OK**. Alternatively, use the **Ctrl-H** keyboard shortcut.

3. Select **OK**.

To hide text and display a symbol where the hidden text is located

1. Select View PrEferences (**Alt-VE**).

2. Turn on **P**aragraph Marks, if necessary, by choosing the check box. You should see an X in the box.

3. Turn off H**I**dden Text, if necessary, by choosing the check box. The check box should be blank.

4. Select **OK**.

To hide text completely

1. Select View PrEferences (**Alt-VE**).

2. Turn off **P**aragraph Marks, if necessary, by choosing the check box. The check box should be blank.

3. Turn off H**I**dden Text, if necessary, by choosing the check box. The check box should be blank.

4. Select **OK**.

Hyphens

Purpose

Enables you to break lengthy words. Hyphenation becomes more important when you are using right-margin justification and narrow column widths.

To hyphenate a document

1. Press **Ctrl-Home** to place the cursor at the beginning of the document.
2. Select **U**tilities **H**yphenate (**Alt-UH**).

   The Hyphenate dialog box contains two check boxes: **C**onfirm and **H**yphenate Caps. With these options, Word confirms each hyphen placement, and the program attempts to place hyphens in capitalized words.
3. Select **OK** from the Hyphenate dialog box.
4. Words shows you all the places where the word can be hyphenated. The hyphen Word proposes to use is highlighted. You can use the arrow keys to position the cursor where you would rather place the hyphen. After you highlight the hyphen you want to use, select **Y**es to confirm the option.
5. Repeat Step 4 until Word finishes hyphenating the document.

   When Hyphenation finishes, the message bar reports the number of words hyphenated.

To use nonbreaking hyphens

1. Type the first word.
2. Press **Ctrl-Shift-hyphen**.
3. Type the second word.

To insert optional hyphens

Press **Ctrl-hyphen.**

Notes

You can create the following kinds of hyphens with Word:

- Use a normal hyphen if you always want the hyphen to appear. Word will break a line, if it must, after the hyphen.
- Use a nonbreaking hyphen if you always want the hyphen to appear, but do not want Word to break a line at the hyphen's location.
- Use an optional hyphen to show Word where to break lengthy words to help even the right margin. Optional hyphens do not appear in the printed text unless they are needed to even the lines.

Importing Spreadsheets

Purpose

Enables you to use tables of data from a spreadsheet program without retyping the data and makes a record of the table's origin after you import the spreadsheet.

To import Lotus or Excel spreadsheets

1. Place the cursor where you want the table to appear.
2. Select **I**nsert **F**ile (**Alt-IF**).
3. In the File **N**ame text box, type the name of the spreadsheet file you want to insert.
4. In the Range list box, type the name of the range, if you are importing a named range. Alternatively, type the range of cells you want to import, using the range expression format the program requires.
5. Select **L**ink so that you can update the table automatically if you later make changes to the spreadsheet.
6. Select **OK**.

To update the table if you later make changes to the spreadsheet

1. Select the table you want to update. If you want to update all the tables in a document at one time, press **Ctrl-5** (on the numeric keypad).
2. Select **I**nsert **F**ile (**Alt-IF**).
3. Select **U**pdate Link without changing anything on the dialog box.
4. Word highlights the table and displays a dialog box asking you to confirm the update of the table. Select **Y**es to update the table.

Indenting Text

Purpose

Enables you to set indents, including left, right, and first line indents.

To indent text with the keyboard

Select Forma**T** **P**aragraph (**Alt-TP**) and select the indent you want in the From Le**F**t, First Li**N**e, or From Ri**G**ht text boxes.

or

Press **Ctrl-N** (indent one tab stop), **Ctrl-T** (hanging indent), or **Ctrl-Q** (indent left and right) keyboard shortcuts.

To indent text with the mouse

1. Place the cursor within the paragraph you want to format, or select two or more paragraphs.
2. Select **V**iew **R**uler (**Alt-VR**) or click the **Ruler** icon (the upside-down T in the right window border) with the left mouse button.
3. Place the pointer on the left or right indent symbols.

4. Hold down the right mouse button and drag the bracket left or right.

To set a first-line indent with the mouse

1. Place the cursor within the paragraph you want to format, or select two or more paragraphs.
2. Select **V**iew **R**uler (**Alt-VR**) or click the **Ruler** icon (the upside-down T in the right window border) with the left mouse button.
3. Place the pointer on the left indent symbol.
4. Hold down the right mouse button and drag the bracket right about one inch so that you can see the first line indent symbol (|).
5. Drag the first line indent symbol to its new location.
6. Drag the left indent bracket back to its original location.

To create a hanging indent

1. Place the cursor in the paragraph you want to format.
2. Press **Ctrl-T** to indent the paragraph one tab stop. Press **Ctrl-T** again to indent the paragraph two tab stops, and so on.

Note

You do not need to indent paragraphs to create a left margin because a one-inch left margin already is included in Word's default margin settings.

Indexing

Purpose

Enables you to create an index and insert the correct page numbers. You can create two types of index entries with Word: concordance and conceptual. A concordance entry is a word in your document that you mark for indexing. A conceptual entry is a word that you embed in the text and mark for indexing.

To mark a concordance entry

1. Place the cursor on the first character of the word you want to index.
2. Press **Ctrl-H**.
3. Type the index code (**.i..**).
4. Place the cursor directly after the word.
5. Press **Ctrl-H** again and type the end mark (**;**).

To mark a conceptual entry

1. Place the cursor just before the text that discusses the concept you want to index.
2. Press **Ctrl-H**.
3. Type **.i.** followed by the conceptual entry and **;**.

To mark a subentry

1. Place the cursor just before the text you want to index.
2. Press **Ctrl-H**.
3. Type the **.i.**, followed by the main entry, a colon (**:**), the subentry, and the end code (**;**).

To create an entry that marks a range of pages

1. At the beginning of the discussion of the topic, insert an entry, using the following coding:

   .i.subject;

2. At the end of the discussion of the topic, insert exactly the same entry.

   Note that the coding must be formatted as hidden text.

To create a cross-reference entry

1. Press **Ctrl-H**.

2. Type **.i.** followed by the term you want cross-referenced, a colon, the word **See**, the index entry to which you want to refer the reader, and the end mark. For example,

   .i.manufacturing:See Industry;

To generate the index

1. Select **I**nsert **I**ndex (**Alt-II**).
2. Select **OK**.

Notes

If you are planning to compile an index for a report of 100 pages or more, you probably will need expanded memory to complete the job. If Word runs out of memory before completing the index, the program cannot complete the job.

Note that if you fail to mark the index code and end mark as hidden text, Word will not remove these codes from the document or print the entry in the index.

See also *Table of Contents*.

Justifying Text

Purpose

Enables you to position text flush with both the left and right margin.

To format a paragraph flush right

1. Place the cursor in the paragraph you want to format. You may select several paragraphs if you want to format more than one paragraph.
2. Select Forma**T** **P**aragraph (**Alt-TP**).
3. Select the **R**ight option button.

   or

   Use the **Ctrl-R** keyboard shortcut.

4. Select **OK**.

To justify a paragraph

1. Place the cursor in the paragraph you want to format. You may select several paragraphs if you want to format more than one paragraph.
2. Select Forma**T** **P**aragraph (**Alt-TP**).
3. Select the **J**ustified option button.

   or

   Use the **Ctrl-J** keyboard shortcut.
4. Select **OK**.

To restore flush left formatting

1. Place the cursor in the paragraph you want to format. You may select several paragraphs if you want to format more than one paragraph.
2. Select Forma**T** **P**aragraph (**Alt-TP**).
3. Select the **L**eft option button.

   or

   Use the **Ctrl-L** keyboard shortcut.

4. Select **OK**.

Key Status Indicator Codes

Purpose

Enables you to work in several operating modes, which are toggled on and off by special keys. When you have toggled the mode on, a code appears on the status line.

Key Status Indicator Codes

Code	*Key or Command*	*Explanation*
CL	**Caps Lock**	Enters all letters as uppercase.
CS	**Ctrl-Shift-F8**	Column select mode.
EX	**F8**	Extend selection mode.
OT	**Ins**	Overtype mode.
LD	**U**tilities **L**ine Draw	Draws lines.
LY	**V**iew **L**ayout	Displays page layout.
MR	**Ctrl-F3**	Records a macro.
MX	**Ctrl-F10**	Maximizes (zooms) the window.
NL	**Num Lock**	Keyboard enters numbers.
RM	**U**tilities Revision **M**arks	Marks revisions.
SL	**Scroll Lock**	Arrow keys scroll screen.
ST	**M**acro **R**un	Runs macro line by (**S**tep) step-by-step.

Line Draw

Purpose

Enables you to create simple illustrations. You must have a printer that can print the IBM extended character set.

To make a simple illustration

1. Position the cursor where you want to start drawing and select Utilities Line Draw (**Alt-UL**).
2. Press the **right-**, **left-**, **down-**, and **up-arrow** keys to draw with the cursor. Press **Home** to draw a line to the left margin, and press **End** to draw a line to the right margin.
3. To move the pen, press **Esc** or click either mouse button. Reposition the cursor, and select Utilities Line Draw again.
4. To correct mistakes, exit Line Draw by pressing **Esc**, and press **Ins** to toggle the Overtype mode on. Delete any unwanted characters.

To change the line draw character

1. Select Utilities CUstomize (**Alt-UU**).
2. Drop down the Linedraw Character list box.
3. Select a line draw character or type the character you want to use.
4. Select **OK**.

Notes

Line Draw is no substitute for a good graphics or illustration program. You can enter only horizontal or vertical lines, and it is easy to make mistakes that are difficult to fix. Worse, the line draw characters are made up of the standard IBM graphics characters, and like any character, they can be disturbed if you enter or delete text.

See also *Borders and Boxes*.

Line Numbers

Purpose

Enables you to perform legal or technical editing in which displaying line numbers may be helpful. Word counts lines per page, starting from the top, excluding page numbers and headers.

To turn on line numbers

1. Select **V**iew Pr**E**ferences (**Alt-VE**).
2. Select the Show Line **N**umbers check box.
3. If you want, select the Count Blan**K** Space check box.
4. Select **OK**.

To print line numbers

1. Place the cursor in the section of the document for which you want line numbers printed.
2. Select Forma**T** **S**ection (**Alt-TS**).
3. Select Add L**I**ne Numbers.

   After you choose this option, Word activates the From Te**X**t and Count **B**y text boxes. By default, Word places the line numbers 0.4-inch to the left of the text and prints line numbers for each line. You can change these options to print line numbers at specified intervals.
4. Select **OK**.

Note

If you are working with a slow computer, think twice about turning on line numbers. With line numbers turned on, Word must recalculate the current line number position every time you move the cursor.

Line Spacing

Purpose

Sets the space between lines. By default, Word uses 12-point line spacing.

To adjust line height automatically to the largest point size you have chosen

1. Select the paragraph that contains a nondefault point size.
2. Select FormaT Paragraph.
3. Drop down the LIne list box in the Spacing field.
4. Select the Auto option.
5. Select **OK**.

To double-space text as you type

1. Select FormaT Paragraph (**Alt-TP**) and type **2 li** in the LIne text box. Alternatively, press **Ctrl-2**.
2. Type the text.

To double-space text after you type

1. Select the text.
2. Select FormaT Paragraph (**Alt-TP**) and type **2 li** in the LIne text box. Alternatively, press **Ctrl-2**.

To restore single line spacing as you type

1. Press **Enter** to start a new paragraph.
2. Select FormaT Paragraph (**Alt-TP**) and type **1 li** in the LIne text box. Alternatively, press **Ctrl-1**.

To restore single-line spacing after you type

1. Select the paragraph.
2. Select FormaT Paragraph (**Alt-TP**) and type **1 li** in the LIne text box. Alternatively, press **Ctrl-1**.

Macros

Purpose

Enables you to store a list of keystrokes that you set in motion with just one keystroke.

Supplied Macros

Word 5.5 comes with a set of 74 prewritten macros. To use the macros that Microsoft supplies with Word, you must merge the MACRO.GLY file into the current glossary.

To open the MACRO.GLY glossary file

1. Open a new, blank document that you can use to experiment with Word's supplied macros.
2. Select **M**acro **E**dit (**Alt-ME**).

   The Edit Macro dialog box is displayed.
3. Select **O**pen Glossary.

   The Open Glossary dialog box is displayed.
4. Select MACRO.GLY in the **F**iles list.
5. Select **OK**.

   Word opens the glossary titled MACRO.GLY, and you see the macros listed in the Edit Macro dialog box.
6. Select **Close**.

To run one of Word's supplied macros

1. Select **M**acro **R**un (**Alt-MR**).
2. Highlight the name of the macro you want to run.
3. Select **OK** or press the macro's keyboard shortcut.

To clear MACRO.GLY and restore the default glossary

1. Select **M**acro **E**dit (**Alt-ME**).
2. Select **O**pen Glossary.

3. Select NORMAL.GLY in the Files list box.
4. Select **OK**.
5. Select **Close**.

To run a macro

Type the glossary's name (such as **Delete_Word_Right**) and press **F3**.

or

Select **M**acro **R**un (**Alt-MR**) and select the macro from the Macros list box.

or

Press the macro's Ctrl-key code to start the macro.

Custom Macros

As you use Word, you surely will think of many steps that you make repeatedly and that you would like to automate with macros. You can create macros by recording them or writing them.

To record a macro

1. Select **M**acro Re**C**ord (**Alt-MC)** or press **Ctrl-F3**.
2. In the **M**acro Name box, type a name for the macro.
3. In the Macro **K**eys box, actually press the keys you want to use to start the macro.
4. Select **OK**.
5. Press the keys you want recorded.
6. Select **M**acro Stop Re**C**order (**Alt-MC**) or **Ctrl-F3** to stop recording the macro.

To test a macro

1. Select **M**acro **R**un (**Alt-MR**).
2. In the Macro **N**ame list box, highlight the name of the macro you want to test.
3. Select **S**tep so that you see an X in the check box.
4. Select **OK**.

5. Press any key besides Esc to move to the next step in the macro.
6. Repeat Step 5 until the macro is finished running.
7. Select **M**acro **R**un (**Alt-MR**) and remove the X from the Step check box.

To write a macro

1. Write the macro in a new, blank Word document.
2. Select the macro.
3. Select **M**acro **E**dit (**Alt-ME**).
4. In the Macro **N**ame box, type a name for the macro.
5. In the Macro **K**eys box, press the keys you want to use to activate the macro.
6. Select **D**efine.

Notes

When you assign a keyboard shortcut to a macro, be careful to avoid duplicating existing keyboard shortcuts. The keyboard shortcuts you assign to macros cancel existing keyboard shortcuts.

Before you record a macro ask yourself these questions:

- What keys must I press to carry out the action successfully?
- Where should the cursor be placed when the macro starts running?
- If the macro changes one of Word's operating modes, do you want to change it back when the macro quits running?
- Does the macro perform any operations that could lose data?

Mailing Labels

See *Form Letters*.

Margins

Purpose

Enables you to set the white space at the top, bottom, left, and right of the printed page. Word uses a one-inch margin on all four sides by default.

To change the margins

1. Select FormaT Margins (**Alt-TM**).

   The Section Margins dialog box is displayed.

2. Select **T**op, and type the new top margin measurement in the text box.

   Measure from the top edge of the page. For example, if you type **1.25"**, Word prints the text 1.25 inches from the top edge of the page.

3. Select **L**eft, and type the new left margin measurement.

4. Select **B**ottom, and type the new bottom margin measurement.

5. Select **R**ight, and type the new right margin measurement.

6. Select **OK**.

To change the default margins

1. Select FormaT Margins (**Alt-TM**), and type the margin measurements that you want for all Word documents.

2. Select **U**se as Default.

3. Select **OK**.

To print margins you choose on odd pages with reversed margins for even pages

1. Select FormaT Margins (**Alt-TM**).

   The Section Margins dialog box is displayed.

2. Select MIrror Margins.

   If you choose a left margin of one-and-one-half inches and a right margin of one inch, Word prints these margins on the odd-numbered pages. On the even-numbered pages, it prints a left margin of one inch and a right margin of one-and-one-half inches.

Note

Remember to distinguish margins from the paragraph indents you can create with the FormaT Paragraph command. A left or right indent adds to the existing margin.

Math

Purpose

Enables you to perform simple arithmetic operations right on the screen.

To add up the numbers in a table's columns

1. Select the upper right corner of the column of data you want to add.
2. Press **Ctrl-Shift-F8** to turn on the Column-select mode.
3. Expand the selection to the right and down to encompass just the numbers in the column.
4. Press **F2**.
5. Press **Esc** to turn off Column select mode.
6. Place the cursor where you want the sum to appear and press **Shift-Ins**.

To calculate a math expression

1. Type an arithmetic expression anywhere in the document.
2. Select the expression.
3. Select Utilities Calculate or press the **F2** keyboard shortcut.
4. Place the cursor where you want to insert the result.
5. Press **Shift-Ins.**

Notes

Word uses the following mathematical operators:

Operator	*Arithmetic Function*
+ (or no operator)	Addition
– (or parentheses)	Subtraction
x	Multiplication
/	Division
%	Percent

Keep the order of evaluation in mind if you create complex expressions. Word evaluates percentages first, followed by multiplication and division operations, and finally addition and subtraction operations.

If you place an expression in parentheses, Word evaluates the expression in parentheses first.

Measurement Options

Purpose

Word measures horizontally in inches and vertically in 12-point lines (six lines to an inch). You can change the unit of measurement to printer's points, metric units, and fixed-font character positions.

To change the default measurement format

1. Select **U**tilities C**U**stomize (**Alt-UU**).

   The Customize dialog box is displayed.

2. Drop down the Measure list box.

3. Scroll the list box until you see the option you want.

   You can choose from the following options:

Abbreviation	*Measurement format*
In or **"**	Inches (default)
Cm	Centimeters
P10	Character positions in Pica fixed-width font (10 characters per inch)
P12	Character positions in Elite fixed-width font (12 characters per inch)
Pt	Printer's points (72 per inch)

4. Select the measurement option. Press **Alt-down arrow** or press **Enter**. If you are using a mouse, click the option with the left mouse button.

5. Select **OK**.

Note

If you omit the measurement code, Word uses the default measurement format. Suppose that you are using the default settings (lines and inches) and you type **14** in the Line Spacing text box of the Paragraph dialog box. Word leaves 14 blank lines between each printed line. To enter a line spacing of 14 points, you must type **14 pt**.

Moving Files

Purpose

Enables you to move to a floppy disk, files that you no longer use on an everyday basis.

To move files to a floppy disk

1. Select **F**ile **F**ile Management (**Alt-FF**).
2. Select the files you want to move.

   You can select the files in the **F**iles list box, or you can perform a **S**earch operation to limit the display to just the files you want to move.
3. Select **C**opy.

   The Copy dialog box is displayed.
4. Select the De**L**ete Files After Copy check box so that you see an X.
5. Use the **D**irectories window to choose the drive or directory to which you want to move the files.
6. Select **OK**.

Note

If Word finds a file on the destination disk with the same file name as the file you are copying, you see an alert box. To overwrite the file, select **OK**. To cancel the copying operation, select **Cancel**.

Moving Text Blocks

Purpose

Enables you to move a block of text from one part of a document to another.

To perform a block move with the keyboard

1. Select the text.

2. Select **E**dit Cu**T** (**Alt-ET**) or use the **Shift-Del** keyboard shortcut.
3. Move the cursor to the place you want the text to appear.
4. Select **E**dit **P**aste (**Alt-EP**) or use the **Shift-Ins** keyboard shortcut.

To perform a block move with the mouse

1. Select the text.
2. Move the pointer to the place you want the text to appear.
3. Hold down the **Ctrl** key and click the right mouse button.

Notes

Users of previous Word versions should note that the Ins key no longer inserts text from the Scrap. You must press **Shift-Ins** to insert text from the Scrap.

See *Scrap*.

Newline

Purpose

Breaks the line without starting a new paragraph. Word regards each line as a paragraph, and you can use any editing or formatting commands to affect all the lines.

To insert a newline command

Press **ShiftEnter**.

Note

Use the Newline command when you want to affect lines of text that are not ordinarily considered paragraphs. For example, this command is useful for formatting poems and return addresses.

Nonbreaking Spaces

Purpose

Enables you to prevent Word from separating two words or breaking a mathematical formula when the program prints a document.

To enter a nonbreaking space

1. Type the first word.
2. Press **Ctrl-Shift-Space bar**.
3. Type the second word.

Note

Remember that the line breaks you see on-screen are not necessarily the ones Word uses when you print. Use a nonbreaking space when you want to make sure that two words are not separated.

Opening Files

Purpose

Enables you to see and use a file you previously created and saved.

To open a document

1. Select **F**ile **O**pen or press **Alt-Ctrl-F2**.
2. Place the highlight bar on the document's file name in the **F**iles window.
3. Select **O**pen or double-click on the file name.

To open a file in a directory other than the default

1. Select **F**ile **O**pen or press **Alt-Ctrl-F2**.
2. Activate the **D**irectories list box.
3. To move out of the default document directory, select the parent directory symbol.

4. Activate the **D**irectories list box again, and scroll the list box to display the name of the directory in which the file is stored.

5. Select the name of the directory in which the file is stored.

6. Activate the **F**iles list and select the file you want to open.

7. Select **OK** or double-click on the file name.

To open a file in a drive other than the default

1. Select **F**ile **O**pen or press **Alt-Ctrl-F2**.

2. Activate the **D**irectories list box.

3. Select the drive name so that you can access a different drive.

4. Activate the **F**iles list and select the file you want to open.

5. Select **OK**.

Outlining

Purpose

Enables you to create outlines before you write a document, while you write it, or after you write it.

To shift to Outline-edit mode

Select **V**iew **O**utline (**Alt-VO**) or press **Shift-F2**.

To return to the document

Select **V**iew **O**utline (**Alt-VO**) or press **Shift-F2**.

To move to the Outline-organize mode

1. If necessary, select **V**iew **O**utline (**Alt-VO**) or press **Shift-F2** to enter the **O**utline-edit mode.

2. Press **Shift-F5**.

To outline an existing document

1. Open the document. If the document lacks a title and headings, add them.
2. Press **Shift-F2** to toggle on the Outline-edit mode.
3. Place the cursor in the first heading.
4. Press **Ctrl-keyboard 9** to define the heading as an outline heading.

   Word defines the first heading as a Level 1 heading.
5. Move the cursor to the next heading. Press **Ctrl-keyboard 9**. Press **Ctrl-0** to lower the heading's level if necessary.

   As you do subsequent headings, you can press **Ctrl-0** to further lower the heading. If you lower a heading too many levels, press **Ctrl-9** to raise the level.
6. Repeat Steps 4 and 5 until you define all the document headings as outline headings.
7. Hide the body text by pressing **Ctrl-keypad 5** and **Shift-keypad-.**
8. Exit the Outline-edit mode by pressing **Shift-F2**.

To type a heading at the current level

Type the heading. If you press **Enter**, you can type an additional heading at the same level.

To lower the heading one level

Press **Ctrl-0**.

To raise the heading one level

Press **Ctrl-9**.

To convert a heading to body text

Press **Ctrl-X**.

To collapse the body text under a single heading

1. Select the heading for which you want to collapse the body text.
2. Press **Shift-keypad-**.

To collapse the subheadings under a heading

1. Place the cursor on the heading above the subheadings you want to collapse.
2. Press **Keypad-**.

To collapse all body text at once

1. Press **Ctrl-keypad 5** to select the whole outline.
2. Press **Shift-keypad-**.
3. Press **Shift-F5** to exit the Outline-organize mode and return to the Outline-edit mode.

To collapse all the subheadings down to a level you specify

Hold down the **Shift** and **Alt** keys and press a number corresponding to the last level you want to display.

To display only the Level 1 headings, press **1**. To display Level 1 and Level 2 headings, press **2**, and so on.

To expand the collapsed subheadings one level below a heading

1. Select the heading below which you want to expand the subheadings one level.
2. Press **keypad+**.

To expand all the subheadings under a heading

1. Select the heading below which you want to expand all the subheadings.
2. Press **keypad*.**

To expand all the headings and subheadings to a level you specify

Hold down the **Shift** and **Alt** keys and press a number corresponding to the last level you want to display.

To display only the Level 1 headings, press **1**. To display Level 1 and Level 2 headings, press **2**, and so on.

To scroll through a lengthy document in the Outline-edit mode

1. Press **Shift-F2** to enter the Outline mode.
2. Hide the body text so that you can see the outline's structure by pressing **Ctrl-keypad 5** and then **Shift-keypad-**.
3. Place the cursor on the heading to which you want to scroll.
4. Press **Shift-F2** again to return to the Document mode.

To select headings in Outline-organize mode

Use the following keys and key combinations to restructure an outline by moving and deleting headings.

Key(s)	*Effect*
Up arrow	Selects preceding heading at the current level.
Down arrow	Selects next heading at current level.
Left arrow	Selects the next heading up, regardless of level.
Right arrow	Selects next heading down, regardless of level.
Home	Selects nearest heading at next higher level above the selected heading.
End	Selects last heading at next lower level below the selected heading.
F8	Selects the current heading and all subheadings and body text below it.
F8-down arrow	Selects the current heading and following headings at the same level.

To number outline headings automatically

1. In the Outline-edit mode, select the first character in the outline.
2. Select **U**tilities **R**enumber.
3. Select **A**ll and make sure that an X appears in the Restart **S**equence check box.
4. Select **OK**.

To remove the numbers Word entered

1. In Outline mode, select the first character of the first heading.
2. Select **U**tilities **R**enumber.
3. Select **R**emove.
4. Select **OK**.

To print an outline

1. Press **Shift-F2** to enter the Outline mode.
2. Hide any body text by pressing **Ctrl-keypad 5** and **Shift-keypad-.**
3. Collapse subheadings to a level you specify by holding down the **Shift** and **Alt** keys and pressing a number corresponding to the lowest outline level you want to display.
4. Select **F**ile **P**rint.

Page Break

Purpose

Enables you to insert manual page breaks in documents.

To insert a manual page break

1. Place the cursor where you want Word to start a new page.

2. Select **I**nsert **B**reak (**Alt-IB**).

   The Break dialog box is displayed with the **P**age button selected.

3. Select **OK**.

   You also can press **Ctrl-Enter** in place of Steps 2 and 3.

To remove a manual page break

1. Place the cursor anywhere on the manual page break.
2. Press **Del**.

Notes

A manual page break looks like a row of dots without spaces. A manual page break differs from an automatic page break, in which the dots are separated by spaces. You also cannot select or position the cursor on an automatic page break, but you can select a manual page break.

Use manual page breaks sparingly, particularly if you plan to do heavy editing. As you delete and insert text above the forced page break, the manual break may become unnecessary.

Page Numbers

See *Headers and Footers*.

Page Size

Purpose

Enables you to print on nearly any size of standard paper, including common European sizes such as A4. You can change the page size for the active document. If you want, you can save new defaults so that all Word documents print on the page size you chose.

To change the page size for the active document

1. Select FormaT Margins (**Alt-TM**).

   The Section Margins dialog box is displayed.

2. Type the new page width.

   The default measurement system is inches.

3. Select the **H**eight text box.

4. Type the new page height.

5. Select **OK** or press **Enter**.

To change the page size defaults for all Word documents

1. Select FormaT Margins (**Alt-TM**) and type a new page width and height.

2. Select **U**se as Default.

3. Select **OK**.

Note

See also *Measurement Options*.

Paragraph Formatting

Purpose

Makes it easy to visualize how text will be arranged on the printed page. Any time you start a new paragraph, you can change these formats. Therefore, it is very easy to create a document that includes both double-spacing and single-spacing, for instance.

To format paragraphs as you type

1. Place the cursor where you want to start typing.

2. Select FormaT Paragraph (**Alt-TP**) and select a paragraph format. Alternatively, use one of the keyboard shortcuts. If you have a mouse, you can set indents on the Ruler.

3. Type the text.

4. Select FormaT Paragraph (**Alt-TP**) and restore the default format. You also can cancel the format by using the same keyboard shortcut again. If you choose an indent, you can cancel the format by moving the indent symbols on the Ruler.

To format paragraphs after you type

1. Select the paragraphs.

2. Select FormaT Paragraph (**Alt-TP**) and choose a paragraph format. Alternatively, use one of the keyboard shortcuts, or, if you are choosing an indent, drag one of the indent symbols on the Ruler.

The Paragraph dialog box

You can choose the following formats in this dialog box:

Format	*Affects Text*
Alignment	Aligns paragraphs within the margin. Left aligns the left margin but leaves the right ragged. Center centers all lines. Right aligns the right margin but leaves the left ragged. Justified aligns both margins.
Indents	Indents paragraphs from margin. If you choose LeFt and type a measurement, Word indents all lines from the left margin by the amount you specified. If you choose First LiNe, Word indents the first line only. RiGht indents all lines of the paragraph from the right margin.

Format	*Affects Text*
Spacing	Affects the way Word spaces lines. If you choose **B**efore, Word inserts one or more blank lines before the paragraph. If you choose **A**fter, Word inserts one or more blank lines after the paragraph.
Side by Side	Aligns selected paragraphs side-by-side on a page, in a special double-column format.
Keep Paragraph	Controls page breaks. Choose Toget**H**er to prevent Word from inserting a page break within the lines of the paragraph. Choose **W**ith Next to prevent Word from inserting a page break between this paragraph and the next one.
Buttons	These dialog boxes contain additional paragraph formats, including custom tab stops, lines and borders, and absolutely positioned text and graphics.

Paragraph Formatting Keyboard Shortcuts

You can use the following keyboard shortcuts in place of choosing from the Paragraph dialog box:

Format	*Shortcut*
Alignment:	
Justified	**Ctrl-J**
Flush-left	**Ctrl-L**
Flush-right	**Ctrl-R**
Centered	**Ctrl-C**

Indentation:

Increase left indent	**Ctrl-N**
Decrease left indent	**Ctrl-M**
Hanging indent	**Ctrl-T**
Indent left and right	**Ctrl-Q**

Line Spacing and Blank Lines:

Blank line before paragraph	**Ctrl-0**
Double line spacing	**Ctrl-2**
Single line spacing	**Ctrl-1**

To repeat a format

1. Select the first instance of the text you want to format.
2. Choose the character or paragraph formatting command.
3. Move the cursor to the next instance of the text you want to format the same way.
4. Select **E**dit **R**epeat (**Alt-ER**) or press **F4**.

To indent a paragraph from the left margin

1. Place the cursor in the paragraph you want to indent.
2. Press **Ctrl-N** to indent the paragraph one tab stop.

   Press **Ctrl-N** again to indent the paragraph two tab stops, and so on.

To decrease the indentation of a stepped paragraph

1. Place the cursor in the indented paragraph.
2. Press **Ctrl-M**.

To cancel an indentation

Press **Ctrl-M** until the text is flush to the left margin, or press **Ctrl-X** to cancel all nondefault paragraph formats.

To search an entire document for formats

1. Press **Ctrl-Home** to position the cursor at the beginning of the document.
2. Select **E**dit **S**earch.
3. In the Search dialog box, select Search for **F**ormatting Only.
4. Select **C**haracter or **P**aragraph.
5. Select the format or formats for which you want to search.
6. Select **OK**.
7. To repeat the search, press **Shift-F4**.

To replace formats throughout an entire document

1. Press **Ctrl-Home** to position the cursor at the beginning of the document.
2. Select **E**dit R**E**place (**Alt-EE**).
3. In the Replace dialog box, choose Replace **F**ormatting Only.
4. Select **C**haracter or **P**aragraph.
5. Select the format or formats that you want Word to remove from the document.
6. Select **R**eplace With.
7. Select the format or formats that you want Word to place in the document.
8. Click **X** to change Replace Selection to Replace All, and then click **Y**.

To cancel paragraph formatting

To cancel paragraph formatting, do one of the following:

- Select Forma**T** **P**aragraph (**Alt-TP**) and change the setting in the Paragraph dialog box.

- Use a different alignment keyboard shortcut (to cancel alignment formats only).
- Press **Ctrl-X** to cancel all nondefault paragraph formats.
- Restore the default indent format on the Ruler.

Notes

If you want to format previously typed paragraphs, you do not need to highlight the whole paragraph if you are selecting just one paragraph. Placing the cursor within the paragraph is sufficient to select it for paragraph formatting purposes.

See also *Indenting Text* and *Ruler*.

Previewing Documents

Purpose

Enables you to preview how a document will look when printed. You can see the whole document, including margins and formatting.

To preview documents before printing

1. Select **F**ile Print Pre**V**iew (**Alt-FV**) or press **Ctrl-F9**.
2. When the preview screen appears, note how the text is laid out relative to the entire page.
3. Select **F**ile E**X**it Preview or press **Esc** to return to the document.

To preview and confirm all page breaks

1. Select **U**tilities Re**P**aginate Now (**Alt-UP**).

   The Repaginate Now dialog box appears.
2. Select **C**onfirm Page Breaks.
3. Select **OK**.

If Word encounters a page break you entered manually, you see the message

```
Press Enter to confirm or the delete
key to remove page break.
```

If Word encounters a page break that Word entered as it paginated your document, you see the message

```
Press Enter to confirm page break or
use direction keys to reposition it.
```

4. Press **Enter** to confirm the page break. Press **Del** to remove a manual page break or press **up arrow** to reposition an automatic page break, and then press **Enter**.

5. Repeat Step 4 until you confirm all page breaks in the document.

Notes

You can use the preview feature to check for common formatting problems. Common problems include the following:

- Do the headers or footers appear in the top or bottom margin? If not, you probably forgot to use Forma**T** **H**eader/Footer to mark the header or footer.

- Are page numbers missing? If you tried to turn on page numbers with the **I**nsert Page N**U**mbers dialog box, you may have forgotten to choose the From **T**op or From **B**ottom option.

- Do paragraphs appear appropriately spaced? If you are printing a single-spaced document, you may find that the document looks more attractive if a blank line appears between paragraphs. Return to the document, select all text paragraphs, and press **Ctrl-0**.

Printer Setup

Purpose

Before you print for the first time, and especially if your printer doesn't work properly with Word, you should check these settings to make sure that they are correct.

To check the printer's settings in the Printer Setup dialog box

1. Select **F**ile P**R**inter Setup (**Alt-FR**).

   The Printer Setup dialog box is displayed.

2. Check that the following information is correct:

   - **P**rinter File
   - Printer **N**ame
   - **C**onnect To
   - Paper F**E**ed

3. When all information is correct, select **OK**. If you do not need to make changes, select **Cancel**.

Printing

Purpose

Enables you to get a hard-copy printout of a document. With Word, you can choose from several print options.

To print a document

1. Select **F**ile **P**rint or press **Shift-F9**.

   The Print dialog box is displayed.

2. Select **OK** to start printing.

To print in the background while you continue to write and edit in Word

1. Select File PRinter Setup (**Alt-FR**).

   The Printer Setup dialog box is displayed.

2. Select Use Print Queue.

   You see an X in the check box.

3. Select **OK**.

4. Open the first document you want to print.

5. Select File Print or press **Shift-F9**.

6. Repeat Steps 4 and 5 for additional documents.

To create an INCLUDE command

1. Place the cursor where you want the INCLUDE instruction to occur.

2. Press **Ctrl-[** to enter a left chevron.

3. Type **include,** followed by a space.

4. Type the file name of the document you want to include.

5. Press **Ctrl-]** to enter a right chevron.

To print documents you chained together by using the INCLUDE command

1. Use the File Open command to load the document containing the INCLUDE instruction.

2. Select File Print Merge.

3. Select Print.

To pause, continue, restart, or cancel queued printing

1. Select File Print Queue (**Alt-FQ**).

   The Print Queue dialog box is displayed.

2. Select Pause to interrupt printing temporarily, Continue to continue printing after you pause, Restart File to start printing from page 1, or Stop Queue to cancel queued printing.

3. Select **OK**.

To print directly from the keyboard

1. Select **F**ile **P**rint or press **Shift-F9**.
2. Select Direct Text in the **P**rint drop-down list box.
3. Select **OK**.

   The Print Direct Text dialog box is displayed.
4. Type the text.
5. Select **P**rint Text.

Printing Options

Purpose

Enables you to select printing options, such as number of copies, paper feed, page range, and other less frequently used options.

To select print options in the Print dialog box

Select **F**ile **P**rint or press **Shift-F9**.

You can choose from the following printing options:

- **P**rint
- **C**opies
- Paper F**E**ed
- P**A**ge Range
- Page**S**
- To

To select print options in the Print Options dialog box

1. Select **F**ile **P**rint or press **Shift-F9**.
2. Select the Options command button.

   The Print Options dialog box is displayed.

You can choose from the following printing options:

Option	*Printing Effect*
Options	Select **D**raft to print a document without microspace justification or graphics. Select D**U**plex to turn on two-sided printing.
Include	Choose Summary **I**nfo to print the summary sheet with the document. Choose **H**idden Text to print text formatted as hidden text.
Graphics	If more than one option is shown, choose a lower resolution for quick printing and the highest resolution for the final draft.

Quitting

Purpose

Enables you to quit Word safely.

To quit Word

1. From the **F**ile menu, select E**X**it Word (**Alt-F4**).

   The program checks each open document to see whether you saved all changes. If you haven't, you see an alert box asking you whether you want to save the changes.

2. Select **Y**es to save changes or **N**o to abandon changes.

Note

Do not quit Word simply by turning off the power while the program still is on-screen. If you turn off the power without quitting Word, the temporary files clutter up your disk and, if you made any configuration choices, these choices are lost.

Redlining

Purpose

Enables you to enter text that appears in a distinctive emphasis of your choice, such as uppercase, boldface, or double-underlined. The text you delete does not disappear; instead, the text displays as strikethrough characters. This feature facilitates collaborative writing.

To turn on the Redlining editing mode

1. Select **U**tilities Revision **M**arks (**Alt-UM**).

   The Mark Revisions dialog box is displayed.

2. Select **M**ark Revisions so that an X appears in the check box.

3. If you want, choose an emphasis for new text.

   By default, Word underlines new text.

4. To display revision bars next to passages that have been edited, select **R**ight (to display the bars in the right margin), **L**eft (left margin), or **O**utside (in two-sided documents, the margin away from the binding).

5. Select **OK**.

   You see the code RM on the status bar.

To search for changes automatically

1. Position the highlight at the beginning of the file.
2. Select **U**tilities Revision **M**arks (**Alt-UM**).
3. Select the **S**earch button.
4. To accept the highlighted revision, select the **A**ccept Revisions button. To reject the revision, select the Undo Re**V**isions button. To skip the highlighted revision and continue the search, select Search.
5. Repeat Steps 3 and 4 until you have accepted or rejected all revisions.

To accept or reject the changes in a selection

1. Select the text.
2. Select **U**tilities Revision **M**arks (**Alt-UM**).
3. Select **A**ccept Revisions or Undo Re**V**isions.
4. Select **OK**.

   If you chose the wrong button, choose **E**dit **U**ndo (**Alt-EU**) or use the **Alt-Backspace** keyboard shortcut immediately.

Renaming Files

Purpose

Enables you to rename files through Word without using DOS.

To rename a file

1. Select **F**ile **F**ile Management (**Alt-FF**).
2. Place the highlight bar on the file you want to rename.
3. Select Re**N**ame.

   The Rename dialog box is displayed.
4. Type the new file name.

   Word automatically deletes the name it proposes (*.DOC).
5. Select **OK**.

   You see the renamed file in the Files list box.

Retrieving Documents

Purpose

Enables you to get existing documents so that you can expand, edit, or print as you want.

To start Word and open a document at the same time

1. At the DOS prompt, activate the Word document directory.

   If your Word document directory is named C:\WORD\DOCS, for example, you type **CD C:\WORD\DOCS** and press **Enter**.

2. Type **word** followed by a space and the file name of the document you want to open.

3. Press **Enter**.

   Word starts and displays the document you named.

To retrieve an existing document with File Open

1. Select **F**ile **O**pen (**Alt-FO**) or use the **Alt-Ctrl-F2** keyboard shortcut.

   The Open dialog box is displayed. In the File **N**ame field, you see the mask (*.DOC) that Word is using to search for your files. Files that conform to the mask are displayed in the **F**iles list box.

2. Select a document in the **F**iles list box.

3. Select **OK**.

To retrieve a document from another directory

1. Select **F**ile **O**pen (**Alt-FO**) or use the **Alt-Ctrl-F2** keyboard shortcut.

   The Open dialog box is displayed.

2. Activate the **D**irectories list box.

   The Directories list box shows your disk's directories, relative to the position of the default directory.

3. Activate a new directory by choosing one of the directory names in the **D**irectories list box.

4. Repeat Step 3 until you find your file.
5. Select **OK**.

Ribbon

Purpose

Shows the current style, font, point size, and character emphasis.

To display the Ribbon

Select **V**iew Ri**B**bon (**Alt-VB**), or point to the ruler icon and click the right mouse button.

The Ribbon contains the following fields:

Field	*Purpose*
Style	Gives you an easy way to see the styles you create and to choose them for formatting purposes.
Font	Enables you to choose any of your printer's fonts.
Pts.	Displays the point sizes your printer can print for the font that is selected.
Emphases	Chooses Bold, Italic, or Underline emphasis. You must have a mouse to choose emphasis on the Ribbon.

To select fonts from the Ribbon

1. Select **V**iew Ri**B**bon to activate the Ribbon.
2. Press **Ctrl-F**, then press **Alt-down arrow** to activate the Font field and pull down the list box. Alternatively, click the Font field's down arrow.
3. Select a font from the drop-down list box.

To select point sizes from the Ribbon

1. Select **V**iew Ri**B**bon to activate the Ribbon.
2. Press **Ctrl-P**, then press **Alt-down arrow** to activate the Pts. field and pull down the list box. Alternatively, click the Pts. field's down arrow.
3. Select a point size from the drop-down list box.

To select bold, italic, or underline emphasis with the mouse

1. Select **V**iew Ri**B**bon to activate the Ribbon.
2. Click **Bld** (Bold), **Ital** (Italic), or **Ul** (Underline).

Note

If you use multiple fonts and point sizes, and especially if you use style sheets, display the Ribbon and become accustomed to using it. The Ribbon is a major convenience and can help you avoid costly printing mistakes.

Ruler

Purpose

Contains symbols that help you understand the format settings for the selected text.

To display the Ruler

Select **V**iew **R**uler (**Alt-VR**) or click the **Ruler** icon (the upside-down T) on the right window border with the left mouse button.

Note

See also *Tabs and Tables*.

Saving

Purpose

Enables you to save your work for future use.

To save a new, unnamed document

1. Select **F**ile Save **A**s (**Alt-FA**) or use the **Alt-F2** keyboard shortcut.

   The Save As dialog box is displayed. The cursor is positioned in the File **N**ame text box. The DOS path that is indicated just above the Directories area should be that of your default document directory.

2. In the File **N**ame text box, type the file name.

3. Select **OK**.

4. In the Summary dialog box, type the document's title in the **T**itle text box.

5. Type the document's author in the **A**uthor text box.

6. Type two or three key words or phrases in the **K**eyword area.

7. Type comments, if you want, in the **C**omments text box.

8. Select **OK**.

To save a document again

Select **F**ile **S**ave (**Alt-FS**) or use the **Alt-Shift-F2** keyboard shortcut.

To turn on Autosave

1. Select **U**tilities C**U**stomize (**Alt-UU**).

   The Customize dialog box is displayed.

2. In the Fre**Q**uency box, type the interval (in minutes) that you want Autosave to save your document to disk.

3. Select **OK**.

Note

Using Autosave is not the same as saving your work with Save or Save As. Autosave merely is a backup procedure to be used in case of a computer crash or power failure. Even if you are using Autosave, you must save your work by saving your files to disk.

Scrap

Purpose

Enables you to store text you have cut or copied from a document.

To delete text to the Scrap

1. Place the cursor anywhere in the text.
2. Select the paragraph.
3. Select Edit CuT (**Alt-ET**) or use the **Shift-Del** keyboard shortcut.
4. Press **Del** to delete the extra paragraph mark.

Screen Colors

Purpose

Enables you to select the on-screen colors of specific elements in Word.

To select an alternate color set

1. Select View PrEferences (**Alt-VE**).
2. Select Colors (**Alt-C**).
3. Select Color Set (**Alt-S**).
4. Drop down the list box by pressing the **down-arrow** key or clicking the arrow to the right of the box.

5. Select a color set option.
6. Select **OK**.

To color individual screen elements

1. Select **V**iew Pr**E**ferences (**Alt-VE**).
2. Select **C**olors (**Alt-C**).
3. Select the element you want to color in the **T**hings to Color list box.
4. Press the letter next to the color you want or click the color.
5. Repeat Steps 3 and 4 until you have chosen all the colors you want.
6. Select **OK**.

To restore the default colors

1. Select **V**iew Pr**E**ferences (**Alt-VE**).
2. Select **C**olors (**Alt-C**).
3. Select Color **S**et (**Alt-S**).

   The Color **S**et box will be blank indicating that you previously chose custom colors.

4. Drop down the list box by pressing the **down-arrow** key or clicking the arrow to the right of the box.
5. Select a color set option.
6. Select **OK**.

Notes

If you work with more than one point size, use the Colors dialog box to find out which colors have been assigned to the various point sizes. Modify these colors so that you can see and understand the point size choices.

See also *Font* and *Windows*.

Scrolling

Purpose

Enables you to bring text that you previously created and which is no longer on the screen into view in the document window.

To scroll with the keyboard

1. Press the **Scroll Lock** key until you see `SL` on the status line.
2. You can use the following scrolling techniques:

- To scroll up one line, press the **up-arrow** key.
- To scroll down one line, press the **down-arrow** key.
- To scroll left one-third of the screen, press the **left-arrow** key.
- To scroll right one-third of the screen, press the **right-arrow** key.

To scroll with the mouse

You can use the following mouse scrolling techniques:

- To scroll up or down one line, click the left mouse button on the up or down scroll arrow.
- To scroll up or down continuously, click and hold down the left mouse button on the up or down scroll arrow.
- To scroll up or down one screen, click the left mouse button on the scroll bar background above or below the scroll box.
- To scroll up or down more than one screen, click the left mouse button on the scroll box and drag up or down.
- To scroll left or right one column, click the left mouse button on the left or right scroll arrow.
- To scroll left or right one-third on the screen, click the left mouse button on the scroll box.

- To scroll left or right more than one screen, click the left mouse button on the scroll box, and drag up or down.

Notes

You cannot move the cursor past the end mark. If you try to move the cursor in a blank document, Word beeps to signal an error.

See also *Cursor-Movement Keys*.

Searching for Text

Purpose

Enables you to specify up to a 254-character search.

To perform a simple search

1. Press **Ctrl-Home** to position the cursor on the first character of the document.
2. Select **E**dit **S**earch (**Alt-ES**).

   The Search dialog box is displayed. The default options initiate a search in the Down direction.
3. Type the search text in the Text to **S**earch for field.
4. Select **OK**.

To perform a case-sensitive search

1. Press **Ctrl-Home** to position the cursor on the first character of the document.
2. Select **E**dit **S**earch (**Alt-ES**).
3. Type the search text in the Text to **S**earch for field.
4. Select the **M**atch Upper/Lowercase check box.
5. Select **OK**.

To perform a whole-word search

1. Press **Ctrl-Home** to position the cursor on the first character of the document.
2. Select **E**dit **S**earch (**Alt-ES**).
3. Type the search text in the Text to **S**earch for field.
4. Select the **W**hole Word check box.
5. Select **OK**.

To replace text

1. Press **Ctrl-Home** to position the cursor on the first character of the document.
2. Select **E**dit R**E**place (**Alt-EE**).

   The Replace dialog box is displayed.
3. In the Text to **S**earch for field, type the search text.
4. In the **R**eplace With field, type the text you want to substitute for the search text.
5. Select the **W**hole Word check box.
6. If you want, select the **M**atch Upper/Lowercase check box.
7. Make sure that the **C**onfirm Changes check box is checked.
8. Select **OK**.
9. Select **Y**es to make the replacement, **N**o to skip this selection and continue searching, or **C**ancel to return to the document.

Note

Avoid searching without confirmation. Word may make substitutions you didn't anticipate.

Sections

Purpose

Enables you to create a document with more than one page format.

To divide a document into two sections

1. Position the cursor where you want the new page style format to begin.
2. Select **I**nsert **B**reak (**Alt-IB**).

   The Break dialog box is displayed.
3. Select the **S**ection option button.
4. Select the type of section break you want.

   You can choose from the following:

Next Page	Starts the section on the next page in the pagination sequence.
Even Page	Starts the section on the next even-numbered page.
Odd Page	Starts the section on the next odd-numbered page.
Con**T**inuous	Begins the new section without a page break.
5. Select **OK**.
6. Position the cursor above the section mark. Choose the page style formats you want for the first section in the document.
7. Position the cursor below the section mark. Choose the page style formats you want for the second section in the document.

To change the page break style after inserting a section mark

1. Place the cursor within the section.

2. Select FormaT Section (**Alt-TS**).
3. Select a page break style from the SEction Start drop-down list box.
4. Select **OK**.

To delete a section mark

1. Place the cursor on the section mark or click next to the selection bar.
2. Press **Del**.

Selecting Files

Purpose

Enables you to perform file management operations through Word.

To select a file

1. Select File File Management (**Alt-FF**).
2. Place the highlight bar on the file.
3. Press the **Space bar**.

To select all the files in the Files list box

Press **Ctrl-Space bar**.

Selecting Text

Purpose

Enables you to highlight text so that you can perform editing or formatting operations.

To select fixed units of text with the F8 key

1. Press **F8**.
2. Press **F8** again until you have selected the amount of text you want.

   The second time you press **F8**, you select the current word. The third time, the current sentence. The fourth time, you extend the selection to the current paragraph. The fifth time you press **F8**, you select the whole document.
3. Press **Esc** to exit the Extend Selection mode.

To select fixed units of text with the mouse

You can use the following techniques to select text with the mouse:

- To select a single word, point to the word and double-click the left mouse button.
- To select a line of text, point to the selection bar and click the left mouse button.
- To select a sentence, point to the sentence, and hold down **Ctrl** and click the left mouse button.
- To select a paragraph, point to the selection bar and double-click the left mouse button.
- To select the entire document, point to the selection bar, and hold down **Ctrl** and click the left mouse button.

  Note that the selection bar is an invisible area (two characters wide) just inside the left window border.

To select fixed units of text with the keyboard

You can use the following techniques to select text with the keyboard:

- To select the current word, press **Alt-F6**.
- To select the current sentence, press **Alt-F8.**
- To select the current paragraph, press **Alt-F10**.
- To select the entire document, press **Ctrl-5** (on the numeric keypad).

To select variable amounts of text with the F8 key

1. Place the cursor on the first character you want selected.
2. Press **F8**.
3. Use the cursor-movement keys to expand the highlight until it covers all the text you want to select.

To select variable amounts of text with the mouse

1. Position the pointer on the first character of text you want to select.
2. Press a button and hold it down. The following techniques can be used:
   - If you hold down the left button, Word expands the selection character by character.
   - If you hold down the right button, the selection expands word by word.
   - If you hold down both buttons, the selection expands sentence by sentence.
3. Move the mouse so that the highlight expands.
4. When the highlight covers all the text you want to select, release the button.

To select variable amounts of text with the Shift key

1. Hold down the **Shift** key and press any key that moves the cursor.
2. When you finish expanding the highlight, release the **Shift** key.

Special Character

Purpose

Enables you to use the built-in set of 254 characters needed for work in European languages.

To enter a special character

1. Press **Num Lock** to activate the numeric keypad.

   You see the code `NL` on the status bar.

2. Hold down the **Alt** key and type the two- or three-letter code.

Note

You can find the code number of a given character by opening the document called CHARTEST.DOC, which is in Word's directory.

Spell

Purpose

Enables you to check the spelling of a document and also detect nonstandard capitalization and repeated words.

To check the spelling of a document

1. Press **Ctrl-Home** to start the spelling checker from the beginning of the document.

   Spell checking begins at the cursor's location.

2. Select **U**tilities **S**pelling (**Alt-US**). Alternatively, use the **F7** keyboard shortcut.

   You see the messages `Loading dictionaries` and `Checking dictionaries` on the message bar. If Word cannot find any misspellings, you see the message `No incorrect words found`. If Word finds a word it cannot match with the words in its dictionaries, you see the Spelling dialog box.

   The Spelling dialog box places the discrepant word in the Not Found area. Word lists several possible corrections in the Suggestions list box.

3. You now have several options:

   - If the word is spelled correctly, select **I**gnore to continue. Note that **I**gnore is the highlighted command button; to select it, press **Enter**.

   - If the word is not spelled correctly, activate the Su**G**gestions list box and use the arrow keys to explore the suggestions. If you see the correct spelling, highlight the word and choose **C**hange. Mouse users can double-click on the correctly spelled word.

   - If you do not see the correct spelling, type the correct spelling in the **R**eplace With text box. Select **C**hange or press **Enter**. You are asked to confirm when the word is not in the dictionary.

   - If the error is one you make frequently, move the highlight in the Su**G**gestions list box to display the correct spelling in the **R**eplace With text box. Alternatively, type the correct spelling in the **R**eplace With text box, and then choose R**E**member Correction.

4. After selecting **C**hange or **I**gnore, you can choose **U**ndo if you decide you made the wrong choice.

   Word displays your last correction again.

5. Repeat Steps 3 and 4 until Word reaches the end of the document. Alternatively, select Cancel or press **Esc** to stop the spelling checker.

   The Spelling window disappears, and you see a message bar informing you how many words were checked, how many corrections were made, and how many words were ignored.

To check the spelling of a word or selection only

1. Select the text.

2. Select **U**tilities **S**pelling (**Alt-US**) or use the **F7** keyboard shortcut.

3. To cancel and redo the last spelling action, select **U**ndo from the Spelling dialog box.

To cancel changes that the spelling checker made

Select **E**dit **U**ndo (**Alt-EU**) immediately after Spelling finishes.

To turn off automatic retrieval of suggested spellings

1. From the Spelling dialog box, select **O**ptions.
2. Select **A**lways Suggest so that the X disappears from the check box.
3. Select **OK**.

To turn off automatic detection of punctuation errors

1. From the Spelling dialog box, select **O**ptions.
2. Select **C**heck Punctuation so that the X disappears from the check box.
3. Select **OK**.

To ignore words typed in capital letters

1. From the Spelling dialog box, select **O**ptions.
2. Select **I**gnore ALL CAPS.
3. Select **OK**.

To add correctly-spelled words to the standard dictionary

1. When Spelling flags a correctly-spelled word, make sure that the Add **T**o dictionary list box contains the Standard option. If it doesn't, select Standard from the Add **T**o Dictionary list box.
2. Select **A**dd.

To create a document dictionary and add words to it

1. When Spelling flags a correctly-spelled word, select Add **T**o Dictionary and select Document from the drop-down list box.
2. Select **A**dd.

To create a user's dictionary and add words to it

1. When Spelling flags a correctly-spelled word, select **O**ptions.

2. In the Spelling Options dialog box, select User Dictionary.
3. Type a DOS file name for the user dictionary in the User dictionary list box.
4. Select **OK**.
5. When the alert box appears, select **OK** to confirm the creation of the user dictionary.
6. From the Spelling dialog box, select Add To Dictionary and select the User option from the drop-down list.
7. Select Add to add a word to the new user dictionary.

Notes

When you add words, you can add them to any of the following supplemental dictionaries:

- Standard dictionary
- Document dictionary
- User dictionary

You are not limited to the number of words you can add to the dictionaries. Because the dictionaries are stored in ordinary document formats, however, lengthy word lists slow down the spelling checker.

If your computer is slow, turn off the Always Suggest option. The spelling checker runs much more quickly, and you still can see suggestions by choosing the Suggest command button in the Spelling dialog box.

Starting Word

Purpose

Starts the program and enables you to create a new, blank document.

To start Word

1. Activate the Word document directory.
2. Type **word** and press **Enter**.

Style Sheets

Purpose

Enables you to create a special Word document that contains the style definitions you want to use.

To view the style name on the Ribbon

1. If you do not see the Ribbon on-screen, select **V**iew Ri**B**bon (**Alt-VB**).
2. Place the cursor in the text whose style name you want to check.
3. Look at the Style box on the Ribbon.

To toggle the Style Bar on

1. Select **V**iew Pr**E**ferences (**Alt-VE**).
2. Select St**Y**le Bar so that an X appears in the check box.
3. Select **OK**.

To change an automatic style in NORMAL.STY

1. Select Forma**T** **D**efine Styles (**Alt-TD**).
2. Select **I**nsert **N**ew Style (**Alt-IN**).
3. Select Character, Paragraph, or Section in the Style **T**ype box.
4. Select the name of the automatic style in the **S**tyle I.D. list box.

You can select from the following styles:

Style Name	*Affects*
Annotation	Paragraph formats of all annotations.
Annotation Ref	Annotation reference mark character format.
Footnote	Paragraph formats of all footnotes/endnotes.
Footnote Ref	Footnote reference mark character format.
Header/Footer	Paragraph formats of all headers and footers.
Heading 1	Paragraph format of heading level 1.
Heading 2	Paragraph format of heading level 2.
Heading 3	Paragraph format of heading level 3.
Heading 4	Paragraph format of heading level 4.
Heading 5	Paragraph format of heading level 5.
Heading 6	Paragraph format of heading level 6.
Heading 7	Paragraph format of heading level 7.
Index 1	Paragraph format of index entry level 1.
Index 2	Paragraph format of index entry level 2.
Index 3	Paragraph format of index entry level 3.

Style Name	*Affects*
Index 4	Paragraph format of index entry level 4.
Line Draw	Line draw character format.
Line Number	Line number character format.
Normal	Default paragraph format.
Normal Section	Default section format.
Page Number	Page number character format.
Summary Info	Summary sheet character format.
Table 1	Paragraph format of table of contents level 1.
Table 2	Paragraph format of table of contents level 2.
Table 3	Paragraph format of table of contents level 3.
Table 4	Paragraph format of table of contents level 4.

5. Select **OK**.
6. Use the Format dialog boxes to change the format.
7. Select **F**ile **S**ave (**Alt-FS**) or use the **Alt-Shift-F2** keyboard shortcut.

To change the key code, remark, or style I.D.

1. Select Forma**T** **D**efine Styles (**Alt-TD**).
2. Select the style you want to modify.
3. Select **E**dit **R**ename Style (**Alt-**Re**N**ame).
4. To change the key code, type the new key code in the **K**ey Code box.
5. To change the remark, type the new remark in the **R**emark box.

6. To change the Style I.D., type the style I.D. in the **S**tyle I.D. box or choose the style I.D. from the list.
7. Select **OK**.
8. Select **F**ile **S**ave (**Alt-FS**) or press **Alt-Ctrl-F2** to save your changes.

To change the formatting you attached to a style definition

1. Select Forma**T** **D**efine Styles (**Alt-TD**).

   The NORMAL.STY style sheet is displayed.
2. Select the style you want to modify.
3. Use the Format command to choose the formats you want.
4. Select **F**ile **S**ave (**Alt-FS**) or press **Alt-Ctrl-F2** to save the changes.

To apply a style using the keyboard shortcut

1. Select the text to which you want the format to apply, or place the cursor where you want to start typing in the format.
2. Hold down the **Shift** and **Ctrl** keys and press the key code you created.

To apply a style using the Ribbon

1. If you do not see the Ribbon, select **V**iew Ri**B**bon (**Alt-VB**).
2. Select the text to which you want the format to apply, or place the cursor where you want to start typing in the format.
3. Press **Ctrl-S** to activate the ribbon.
4. Press the **Tab** key to move to the style field you want.

   or

   Click on the style you want with the left mouse button.
5. Type the name of the style you want to apply, or choose the name of the style from the drop-down list box.

To apply a style using the Apply Style dialog box

1. Select the text to which you want the format to apply, or place the cursor where you want to start typing in the format.
2. Select FormaT Apply StYle (**Alt-TY**).
3. To choose the style, select the name in the Style I.D. list box or type the key code in the Key Code box.
4. Select **OK**.

To create a user-defined style

1. Select FormaT Define Styles (**Alt-TD**).
2. Select Insert New Style (**Alt-IN**).
3. In the Key Code box, optionally type the key code you want to apply to the style.
4. In the Remarks box, type a short description of the style.
5. In the Style Type box, choose from Character, Paragraph, or Section.
6. In the Style I.D. box, scroll down the list and choose one of the numbered I.D.s.
7. Select **OK**.
8. Use the Format command's dialog boxes to choose the styles you want.
9. Select File Save (**Alt-FS**) or use the **Alt-Shift-F2** keyboard shortcut.
10. To return to the document, click the close box or select File Close (**Alt-FC**).

To record a style

1. Open the documentation that contains the text with the format you want to record.
2. Select the text.
3. Select FormaT Record Style (**Alt-TR**).
4. In the Key Code box, type the keyboard shortcut you want to use.

5. In the Style **T**ype area, select the style type (character, paragraph, or section).
6. In the **R**emark area, type a brief description of the style.
7. Select **OK**.
8. To see the style in the style sheet, select Forma**T** **D**efine Styles (**Alt-TD**).
9. Select **F**ile **S**ave (**Alt-FS**) to save the style sheet.
10. Select **F**ile **C**lose (**Alt-FC**) or click the close box to close the style sheet and return to the document.

To create a custom style sheet

1. Select **F**ile **N**ew (**Alt-FN**).
2. Select **S**tyle Sheet in the Type area.
3. Select **OK**.

To attach a custom style sheet when you create a document

1. Select **F**ile **N**ew (**Alt-FN**).
2. Select **U**se Style Sheet.
3. Select the style sheet you want to use.
4. Select **OK**.

To attach a custom style sheet to an existing document

1. Open the document and display it on-screen.
2. Select Forma**T** **A**ttach Style Sheet (**Alt-TA**).
3. Select the style sheet you want to use from the **F**iles box.
4. Select **OK**.

To copy styles

1. Open the style sheet to which you want to copy the styles.
2. Select **F**ile **O**pen (**Alt-FO**).
3. Select **S**tyle Sheets in the Show Files area.

4. Select the name of the style sheet from which you want to copy the styles.
5. Select **OK**.
6. Select the style or styles you want to copy.
7. Select **E**dit **C**opy (**Alt-EC**) or use the **Ctrl-Ins** keyboard shortcut.
8. Close the style sheet by clicking the close box or selecting **F**ile **C**lose (**Alt-FC**).
9. To insert the style, select **E**dit **P**aste (**Alt-EP**) or use the **Shift-Ins** keyboard shortcut.

To merge style sheets

1. Open the style sheet to which you want to merge another style sheet.
2. Select **I**nsert **S**tyle Sheet (**Alt-IS**)
3. Select the name of the style sheet you want to insert from the Files list box.
4. Select **OK**.

Summary Sheets

Purpose

Enables you to take advantage of Word's file management features to the maximum. You can reduce the scope of Word's search so that the Files list displays only the documents that conform to criteria you specify.

To fill out a summary sheet

The first time you save a document with **F**ile **S**ave, Word displays a blank summary sheet. The summary sheet contains the following items:

Text Box Name	*Description*
Title	A short version of the document's title.
Author	Use this text box if your computer is used by several people.
Version Number	Keeps track of the versions of a document.
Operator	Use this text box if you are typing someone else's document.
Date CReated	Word fills in this text box automatically.
Date Saved	Word fills in this text box automatically.
Keywords	Use this text box to enter a short description of the document's contents.
Comments	Use this text box to add text that might help you identify the contents of a document.

To update a summary sheet for a document

1. Select File File Management (**Alt-FF**).
2. In the Files window, place the highlight bar on the file that contains the summary sheet you want to update.
3. Select SUmmary.
4. Select **OK**.

Superscript and Subscript

Purpose

Enables you to position text slightly above (superscript) or below (subscript) the text line. Superscripts and subscripts are used extensively for creating footnotes, scientific notation, and mathematical formulas.

To position text slightly below the line

1. Select the text.
2. Select FormaT Character (**Alt-TC**).
3. Select the Subscript option button. Alternatively, use the **Ctrl-=** keyboard shortcut.

To position text slightly above the line

1. Select the text.
2. Select FormaT Character (**Alt-TC**).
3. Select the Superscript option button. Alternatively, use the **Ctrl-+** (or **Ctrl-Shift-=**) keyboard shortcut.

Table of Authorities

Purpose

Enables you to cite authorities by appending to the end of the document a list of statutes, cases, or other authorities cited. This list usually includes page references. To assist you with tables of authorities, Word supplies two macros, authority_entry.mac and authority_table.mac, which you can use to mark authorities and to generate a table of authorities.

To mark a citation the first time you type it

1. Place the cursor where you plan to type the citation.
2. Select Macro Run (**Alt-MR**).

   The Run Macro dialog box is displayed.

3. Highlight `authority_entry` in the Macro **N**ame list box.

4. Select **OK**.

5. When you see the message `Type the new citation`, highlight it and press **Enter**.

   You type the citation in the document, but Word formats the citation as hidden text.

6. When you see the message `What is the source?`, choose a number from the list.

   - **1** = Previous Case
   - **2** = Statute
   - **3** = Regulation
   - **4** = Other

   If you select 4, Word asks you to name the category of this citation.

7. When you see the message `Move the cursor to the beginning of this citation`, press the **up-** and **left-arrow** keys to expand the highlight so that the whole citation is selected. Press **Enter**.

8. Select a name that Word can use to store this citation in a glossary.

   Word stores the citation, complete with all the formatting needed for the table of authorities, in the glossary you created.

To mark the second and subsequent instances of the citation

1. Place the cursor where you want the citation to appear.

2. Select **E**dit Gl**O**ssary (**Alt-EO**).

3. Select the glossary entry you created for the citation in Step 8 of the preceding series of steps.

4. Select **I**nsert.

To compile the table of authorities

1. Select **M**acro **R**un (**Alt-MR**).

   The Run Macro dialog box is displayed.

2. Highlight `authority_table` in the Macro **N**ame list box.

3. Select **OK**.

   Word creates a table of authorities and places the table at the end of the document. You can format this table as needed.

Note

See also *Macros*.

Table of Contents

Purpose

Enables you to generate a table of contents and insert the correct page numbers.

To create a table of contents from an outline

1. Select **V**iew Pr**E**ferences (**Alt-VE**) and remove the X from the H**I**dden Text check box.

   The pagination will be inaccurate if hidden text is visible.

2. Select **V**iew **O**utline (**Alt-VO**) or press **Shift-F2** to switch to the outline view of the document.

3. Hold down the **Shift** and **Alt** keys and then press a number key corresponding to the lowest level of headings you want to include in the table of contents.

   Suppose, for example, that you want to create a table of contents that includes only first-level headings. Press **Shift-Alt-1**. To create a table of contents that includes first-, second-, and third-level headings, press **Shift-Alt-3**.

4. Select **I**nsert Table of **C**ontents (**Alt-IC**).

   The Table of Contents dialog box is displayed. By default, Word compiles the outline from codes, indents each level by 0.4-inch, shows page numbers, and separates the page numbers from the entry by a default tab. You can change the formatting settings.

5. Select **O**utline.

6. Select **OK**.

   Word compiles the table of contents and places it at the end of the document.

To code table of contents entries

You must distinguish between three parts of a completely marked table of contents:

- The Table of contents code (**.c.**) tells Word the text that follows this code is a table of contents entry.
- The heading includes the text you want to print. Do not format the heading as hidden text.
- The end mark (**;**) tells Word where the table of contents entry stops.

To mark headings as you type

1. Place the cursor where you want the heading to appear and press **Ctrl-H**.
2. Type the table of contents code (**.c.**).
3. Press **Ctrl-H** again to toggle hidden text off.
4. Type the heading.
5. Press **Ctrl-H** to toggle hidden text on again.
6. Type the end code (**;**).

To mark headings after you type the headings

1. Place the cursor at the beginning of the heading and press **Ctrl-H**.
2. Type the table of contents code (**.c.**).

3. Place the cursor on the space following the heading and press **Ctrl-H**.

4. Type the end code (**;**).

To code headings at lower levels

You use second-level codes for subject headings within chapters, third-level codes for sections with the second-level units, and so on. Use the following codes for second and other subordinate levels:

Level	*Code*
First	**.c.**
Second	**.c.:**
Third	**.c.::**
Fourth	**.c.:::**
Fifth	**.c.::::**

To compile the table of contents from manually marked headings

1. Select **V**iew Pr**E**ferences (**Alt-VE**) and remove the X from the H**I**dden Text check box.

2. Select **OK**.

3. Select **I**nsert Table of **C**ontents (**Alt-IC**).

4. Select **C**odes, if it is not selected already.

5. Select **OK**.

To recompile the table of contents after making changes

1. Select **I**nsert Table of **C**ontents (**Alt-IC**).

2. Select **O**utline or **C**odes, and alter the default formats, if you want.

3. Select **OK**.

4. Select **Y**es to replace the existing table of contents.

Note

If you are assembling a document in which the front matter is paginated with lowercase Roman numerals, move the table of contents to the front of the document on-screen. Add a title page and other front matter to the section containing the table of contents. Do not forget to format the body text section so that page numbering begins with page 1 in Arabic numbers.

Tabs and Tables

Purpose

Moves the cursor across the screen so that you can set up tabular columns. The preset tab measurement is 0.5". With this setting, tab stops appear every half inch across the screen.

To set new default tab stops for an entire document

1. Select **U**tilities C**U**stomize (**Alt-UU**).
2. Select De**F**ault Tab.
3. Type the new default tab width.
4. Select **OK**.

To set a custom tab with the keyboard

1. Select the paragraph or paragraphs to which you want to apply the custom tabs.
2. Press **Shift-Ctrl-F10** to place the cursor on the Ruler.
3. Press the **right-** and **left-arrow** keys to move the cursor where you want the tab stop to appear. You also can press **PgDn** to move the cursor one inch to the right and **PgUp** to move the cursor one inch to the left.
4. Select the tab alignment you want by pressing the first letter of the alignment (**L**eft, **C**entered, **R**ight, **D**ecimal, or **V**ertical).

5. If you want to add a leader to the tab stop, press the character corresponding to the leader you want to enter.

6. Repeat Steps 3, 4, and 5 to enter more tabs.

7. Press **Enter** to return to the document.

To set custom tabs with the mouse

1. With the ruler displayed, select the paragraph or paragraphs to which the tab stops are to apply.

2. If you want an alignment other than flush left, click the **L** next to the left indent marker on the ruler until it displays the alignment code you want.

3. To select a leader character, click the space left of the L on the ruler line until the leader you want appears.

4. Click the ruler where you want the tab stop.

5. Repeat Steps 2 through 4 to set additional tabs.

To set custom tabs with precise measurement

1. Select the paragraph or paragraphs containing the tab you want to set.

2. Select Forma**T** **T**abs (**Alt-TT**).

3. Type the measurement in the **T**ab Position text box.

4. Select Alignment.

5. Select the Leader, if any.

6. Select **OK**.

To move custom tab stops with the keyboard

1. Select the paragraph or paragraphs that contain the tab or tabs you want to move.

2. Press **Shift-Ctrl-F10** to activate the Ruler.

3. Press the **down arrow** to move to the next tab stop right, and press the **up arrow** to move to the next tab stop left.

4. When you have highlighted the tab you want to move, press **Ctrl-right arrow** to move the tab right, or **Ctrl-left arrow** to move the tab left.

5. Repeat Steps 3 and 4 to move other tabs.
6. Press **Enter** to return to the document.

Special keys used in setting custom tabs

Key	*Effect with format tab set*
Shift-Ctrl-F10	Place cursor on Ruler.
Down arrow	Select next tab stop right.
Up arrow	Select next tab stop left.
Right arrow	Move highlight right on ruler.
Left arrow	Move highlight left on ruler.
PgUp	Move highlight one inch left on Ruler.
PgDn	Move highlight one inch right on Ruler.
Del	Delete custom tab stop.
Ctrl-Del	Delete custom tab stop and all custom tab stops to right of cursor.

To move custom tabs with the mouse

1. Select the paragraph or paragraphs that contain the tab or tabs you want to move.
2. Move the pointer to the tab stop on the Ruler.
3. Hold down the left mouse button and drag the tab stop letter to its new location.
4. Release the mouse button.
5. Repeat Steps 3 and 4 to move additional tab stops.

To delete custom tab stops with the keyboard

1. Select the paragraph or paragraphs containing the custom tab you want to delete.
2. Press **Shift-Ctrl-F10** to place the cursor on the Ruler.

3. Press the **down arrow** to move to the next tab stop right, and press the **up arrow** to move to the next tab stop left.

4. When you have highlighted the tab you want to delete, press **Del** to delete this tab, or press **Ctrl-Del** to delete this tab and all tab stops that appear to the right of the current tab.

5. Repeat Steps 3 and 4 to delete additional tabs.

6. Press **Enter** to return to the document.

To delete custom tabs with the mouse

1. Select the paragraph or paragraphs containing the custom tab you want to delete.

2. On the Ruler, point to the tab stop letter you want to delete.

3. Drag the letter below the Ruler and release the mouse button.

4. Repeat Steps 3 and 4 to delete additional tabs.

To reverse the position of columns in a two-column table

1. Select the character at the upper left corner of the column you want to move.

2. Press **Ctrl-Shift-F8** to turn on the Column-select mode.

3. Extend the selection to the right and down to encompass the column. Be sure to include all tab stops that come after the text in the column.

4. Select **E**dit Cu**T** (**Alt-ET**) or press **Shift-Del** to cut the column to the Scrap.

5. Make sure that each line of data in the new left column ends with a tab character before the paragraph mark.

6. Select the paragraph mark where you want the column to be inserted.

7. Select **E**dit **P**aste (**Alt-EP**) or press **Shift-Ins** to insert the column at the cursor's location.

To move a column left or right

1. Select all the lines you want to move.
2. Move the tab stop that aligns the column.

Notes

Avoid aligning text with spaces. If you use spaces to align text, Word may not print the text aligned properly. If you align text with spaces, proportionally spaced type will look misaligned when you print the document.

See also *Tabs and Tables*.

Thesaurus

Purpose

Supplies synonyms for words that you highlight in a document. Because Thesaurus is organized by 15,000 root words, it is rare to find no synonyms for the word you highlight.

To look up a word in Thesaurus

1. Highlight the word you want to look up.
2. Select **U**tilities **T**hesaurus (**Alt-UT**) or use the **Shift-F7** keyboard shortcut.
3. Choose the sense of the word in the **D**efinitions list box.
4. Highlight the synonym you want and select **R**eplace. If you do not find a word you want, select Cancel.

To see synonyms of words in a Thesaurus list

1. Highlight the word in the **D**efinitions or S**Y**nonyms list box.
2. Select **S**ynonyms.

3. To place one of the words in your document, highlight the word, and choose Replace. Alternatively, repeat Step 2, select Original to display the synonym list of the first word you looked up, or select Cancel to return to the document.

To look up synonyms for a word you do not see in the Thesaurus window

1. Type the word in the Synonyms For text box.
2. Select Synonyms.
3. To place one of the words in your document, highlight the word, and choose Replace. Alternatively, repeat Step 2, select Original to display the synonym list of the first word you looked up, or select Cancel to return to the document.

Windows

Purpose

Enables you to view a document through a frame. With Word 5.5, you can view several windows at one time.

To switch between two or more windows on-screen using the menus

1. Select Window (Alt-W).
2. Select the name of the document to which you want to switch.

To copy or move text between two documents

1. Open the document to which you want to copy or move text.
2. Open the document from which you want to copy or move text.
3. Find the text, highlight it, and use Edit Copy or Edit CuT.

4. Select the first document's name from the **W**indow menu.

5. Move the cursor to the place you want the text to appear.

6. Select **E**dit **P**aste.

To maximize a window using the menu and keyboard

Select **W**indows Ma**X**imize (**Alt-WX**) or press the **Ctrl-F10** keyboard shortcut.

To maximize a window using a mouse

Click the maximize icon, which is the arrow pointing both ways at the top of the right scroll bar.

To size a window with the keyboard

1. Select **W**indow **S**ize (**Alt-WS**) or press the **Ctrl-F8** keyboard shortcut.

2. Use the arrow keys to resize the window. Press the **left** or **right arrow** to change the width. Press the **up** or **down arrow** to change the height.

3. Press **Enter** when the window is the appropriate size.

To size a window with the mouse

1. Position the pointer on the size icon in the lower right corner of the window.

2. Drag the size icon until you are satisfied with the window's size.

3. Release the mouse button.

To move a window using the keyboard

1. Place the cursor in the window you want to move.

2. Select **W**indows **M**ove (**Alt-WM**) or press the **Ctrl-F7** keyboard shortcut.

3. Use the arrow keys to move the window to its new location.

4. Press **Enter** when you are satisfied with the window location.

To display two different documents at the same time

1. Open the first document.
2. Size the first document's window so that it fills only the top half of the screen.
3. Move the window to the bottom half of the screen.
4. Open the second document.
5. Size the second document's window so that it fills only the top half of the screen.

To open an additional window on the same document

1. Place the cursor in the document for which you want to open a new window.
2. Select **W**indow **N**ew Window (**Alt-WN**).
3. Size or move the windows so that you can see both windows at once.

To divide a window into two panes with the keyboard

1. Select **W**indow Spli**T** (**Alt-WT**).
2. Press the **down arrow** to move the split bar down the window.
3. Press **Enter** when you are satisfied with the split appearance.

To move the cursor from one pane to another pane

Press **F6**.

To remove the split with the keyboard

1. Select **W**indow Spli**T** (**Alt-WT**).
2. Press the **up arrow** to move the split bar to the top of the window.
3. Press **Enter**.

To divide a window into two panes with the mouse

1. Place the pointer on the split bar icon.
2. Press the left mouse button and drag the split bar icon down the scroll bar.

3. Release the mouse button when you are satisfied with the split's location.

To move the cursor to another pane with the mouse

Click the mouse anywhere in the pane you want to activate.

To remove the split with the mouse

1. Place the pointer on the split bar icon.
2. Drag the split bar to the top of the scroll bar and release the button.

KEYBOARD SHORTCUTS

The following section lists the keyboard shortcuts that are available with Microsoft Word 5.5.

To get help

F1	Help

To use menus and dialog boxes

F10 or **Alt**	Activate menu bar
Alt-bold letter	Choose command
Bold letter of menu option	Choose option from menu
Tab	Move to next option or dialog box
Alt-down arrow	Open drop-down list box
Alt-up arrow	Close drop-down list box
Enter	Confirm settings and close dialog box
Esc	Cancel command and close dialog box

To move the cursor

Down arrow	Move cursor down one line
Up arrow	Move cursor up one line
Right arrow	Move cursor right one character
Left arrow	Move cursor left one character
Home	Move cursor to beginning of line
End	Move cursor to end of line
Ctrl-right arrow	Move cursor to next word
Ctrl-left arrow	Move cursor to preceding word
PgDn	Move cursor down one screen
PgUp	Move cursor up one screen
Ctrl-PgDn	Move cursor to bottom of window
Ctrl-PgUp	Move cursor to top of window
Ctrl-down arrow	Move cursor to next paragraph
Ctrl-up arrow	Move cursor to preceding paragraph
Ctrl-End	Move cursor to end of file
Ctrl-Home	Move cursor to beginning of file
Ctrl-Shift-F10	Move cursor to Ruler to set tabs
Alt-F1	Move cursor to next field in form
Shift-Alt-F1	Move cursor to previous field in form

To move the cursor in Layout View only

Ctrl-up arrow	Move cursor to beginning of paragraph

Alt-keypad 5-right arrow	Move cursor to next column right
Alt-keypad 5-left arrow	Move cursor to next column left
F5	Go to page, bookmark, annotation, or footnote

To select text

Shift-left arrow	Select character left
Shift-right arrow	Select character right
F8 (twice) or **Alt-F6**	Select current word
Alt-F6 (twice)	Select next word
Shift-End	Select to end of line
F8 (three times) or **Alt-F8**	Select current sentence
F8 (four times) or **Alt-F10**	Select current paragraph
Ctrl-Shift-F8	Select column
Ctrl-keypad 5 or **F8** (five times)	Select entire document
Esc	Cancel extend selection
Shift-F8	Reduce selection

To create and edit text

Enter	Start new paragraph
Shift-Enter	Start new line
Alt-F7	Display line break
Shift-F7	Open Thesaurus
Ctrl-Shift-Enter	Start new column

Ctrl-Enter	Start new page
Ctrl-Shift-hyphen	Insert nonbreaking hyphen
Ctrl-Shift-Space bar	Insert nonbreaking space
Ctrl-hyphen	Insert optional hyphen
Shift-F3	Toggle uppercase/lowercase
Del	Delete character
Backspace	Delete character left
Ctrl-Backspace	Delete word left
Shift-Del	Delete selection to Scrap
Ctrl-Ins or **Alt-F3**	Copy selection to Scrap
Shift-Ins	Insert text from Scrap
Ins or **Alt-F5**	Toggle Insert/Overtype mode
F4	Repeat last editing action
Shift-F4	Repeat last search
Alt-Backspace	Undo
F7	Check spelling

To format characters

Ctrl-B	Bold
Ctrl-I	Italic
Ctrl-U	Underline
Ctrl-D	Double underline
Ctrl-K	Small caps
Ctrl-=	Subscript

Ctrl-+ or **Ctrl-Shift-=**	Superscript
Ctrl-H	Hidden text
Ctrl-P	Choose point size
Ctrl-S	Assign style
Press command again	Cancel a character format
Ctrl-Space bar	Cancel all character formatting
Ctrl-Z	Cancel emphasis and position choices only

To format paragraphs

Ctrl-1	Single line spacing
Ctrl-2	Double line spacing
Ctrl-C	Centered alignment
Ctrl-L	Flush-left alignment
Ctrl-R	Flush-right alignment
Ctrl-J	Justified alignment
Ctrl-T	Hanging indent
Ctrl-Q	Indent both left and right
Ctrl-N	Nest paragraph one tab stop
Ctrl-M	Unnest paragraph one tab stop
Ctrl-X	Cancel paragraph formatting

To use command shortcuts

Ctrl-Ins	Edit Copy
Shift-Del	Edit CuT
F5	Edit Go To

Shift-Ins	Edit Paste
F4	Edit Repeat
Alt-Backspace	Edit Undo
Alt-F4	File EXit Word
Ctrl-F1 or **Alt-Ctrl-F2** or **Ctrl-F12**	File Open
Ctrl-F9	File Print PreView

Index

G

H

I

J

K

L

M

N

O

P

U

W